THE VALIANT WOMEN OF THE VIETNAM WAR

THE
VALIANT
WOMEN
OF THE
VIETNAM
WAR

KAREN ZEINERT

The Millbrook Press
Brookfield, Connecticut

Published by The Millbrook Press, Inc.
2 Old New Milford Road
Brookfield, Connecticut 06804

www.millbrookpress.com

Cover photograph courtesy of Reuters/Corbis-Bettmann

Photographs courtesy of © Vietnam Women's Memorial Project,
Inc./Glenna Goodacre, sculptor/Gregory Staley, photographer: p.2;
Lambert/Archive Photos: p. 17; Photographs and Prints Division,
Schomburg Center for Research in Black Culture, The New York
Public Library, Astor, Lenox and Tilden Foundations: p. 18; National
Archives: pp. 23, 36; Agence France Presse/Archive Photos: p. 26;
Corbis/Bettmann-UPI: pp. 29, 51, 69, 71, 72, 76; Women in Military
Service for America Memorial Foundation, Inc.: p. 32; AP/Wide World
Photos: pp. 39, 78, 87; Pam Koch: p. 42; American Red Cross: p. 46;
State Historical Society of Wisconsin: p. 55; Hulton Getty/Liaison
Agency: p. 62; Library of Congress: p. 66. Map by Joe LeMonnier.

Library of Congress Cataloging-in-Publication Data
Zeinert, Karen.
The valiant women of the Vietnam War / Karen Zeinert.
p. cm.
Includes bibliographical references (p.   ) and index.
ISBN 0-7613-1268-4 (lib. bdg.)
1. Vietnamese Conflict, 1961-1975—Women—United
States. I. Title.
DS559.8.W6Z45   2000   959.704'3'082—dc21
99-24630   CIP

CONTENTS

*It was . . . 1965 when I graduated. At that time,
there wasn't much news about Vietnam. I didn't
know what was going on there. I had no idea that
Vietnam was going to be a major part of my life.*

MARY STOUT, U.S. ARMY NURSE

IN THE BEGINNING 1

"I was asleep," Lieutenant Colonel June Hilton later recalled, "but that loud flat WHAP! WHAP! sound when the first mortars hit the base jolted me awake immediately. In only a minute or two, all of Tan Son Nhut looked ablaze. I've never seen that much [shelling] and it was terrifyingly close."[1]

The shelling at Tan Son Nhut was only one of many surprise attacks during the war in Southeast Asia between what was then known as North and South Vietnam. Throughout this long, bloody conflict (1954–1975), during which the United States supported the South, the North Vietnamese often launched attacks late at night, when their enemies were least prepared to defend themselves.

Danger was not limited to midnight shellings, though, nor was it restricted to attacks from the North Vietnamese. Thousands of South Vietnamese—men, women, and even children—supported North Vietnam. These supporters, eventually known as the Viet Cong, waged a guerrilla war, a series of hit-and-run attacks against their enemies. The Viet Cong targeted government officials, hid explosives in bread baskets in army cafeterias, and tossed grenades into groups of Americans whenever the guerrillas saw an opportunity to do so. They also attacked U.S. and South Vietnamese soldiers when they could and then fled into the countryside or disappeared into an ever-expanding network of tunnels that they had constructed to make escape easier. When American soldiers hacked their way through hot, steamy jungles looking for the guerrillas, the Viet Cong ambushed them.

Because attacks could occur any time in any place, the guerrilla war was very frightening. Judy Jenkins, a volunteer in Vietnam at that time, said, "The knowledge that . . . everywhere was a combat zone was a hard thing to live with day in and day out. The war was with you all the time. . . . Everyone felt it."[2]

In the beginning, many Americans at home were unaware of what was happening in Vietnam simply because there was little information about the conflict in newspapers or on televised news programs. This was due, in part, to the fact that American officials believed the conflict was winnable by the South Vietnamese. These officials assured the media and the public that there was nothing noteworthy occurring in Vietnam, nor was there any cause for alarm. For a while, this low-key approach was accepted.

But when the war heated up and U.S. soldiers were sent to Asia to help the South Vietnamese, the media and the public became concerned. As a result, the war began to make headlines. And when coffins bearing the corpses of American soldiers who had died in Vietnam began to arrive in the United States, the public started to question the war. What, Americans wondered aloud, were U.S. troops doing in Vietnam? And what exactly was this war all about?

This war was like many others in which the Vietnamese had fought during their two-thousand-year history. The first battles began shortly after some of the Viet people were conquered by the Chinese in 208 B.C. As the Chinese expanded their rule, proud

Vietnamese revolted whenever possible. It took them more than a thousand years to convince the Chinese to leave, but convince them they did, and Vietnam became an independent nation.

The mid-1800s was a time of empire building by European nations. France, impressed by Vietnam's lush landscape, rich soil, and potential mineral resources, claimed the country as one of its Asian colonies. The Vietnamese put up such a spirited resistance that it took the French almost thirty years to conquer all of this country of about 130,000 square miles (336,700 square kilometers), which is approximately the size of the state of New Mexico.

World War II brought another invader to Vietnam, the Japanese. In 1940, shortly after the war began, heavily armed Japanese troops were given permission by the French government to occupy France's colonies in Asia and to use some of their ports for military purposes as Japan tried to extend its control over all of Asia. The French government then was under the control of Nazi Germany, a Japanese ally during the war. The Vietnamese struggled against the Japanese with little success. However, at the end of the war in 1945, the defeated Japanese, like the Germans and their other ally, Italy, were forced to abandon all the territory that they had occupied.

A new French government then restated its country's old colonial claim to Vietnam, believing that the colony was still of great economic importance. But the Vietnamese had had enough of foreign rulers. Instead of accepting France's claim, Vietnamese leaders announced that their homeland was now an independent nation. French leaders responded to that statement by sending troops to Vietnam to show who was in charge.

The Vietnamese, led by Ho Chi Minh, repeatedly attacked the French soldiers. After nine years of bitter fighting and a stunning Vietnamese victory at Dien Bien Phu in 1954 (approximately five thousand French soldiers were either killed or wounded, and at least ten thousand were taken prisoner), the French were forced to abandon Vietnam.

Although the Vietnamese were united while fighting the French, after they had achieved victory serious differences developed among some of the leaders, several of whom had very different plans for Vietnam. To avoid more bloodshed, a special meeting was held in 1954 in Geneva, Switzerland, to discuss Vietnam's future.

Eventually world leaders decided to divide Vietnam at the 17th parallel (latitude). Ho Chi Minh would rule the North. His capital would be Hanoi. Ngo Dinh Diem would lead the South, and he would establish his government's headquarters in Saigon. The Vietnamese people were allowed to move from one section to another, and thousands chose to do so. Officials in Geneva also decided that elections would be held in two years. The country would then be reunited and led by the winning candidate. Most believed that it would be Ho Chi Minh because he was a well-known and highly respected war hero.

The United States government was horrified at the thought of Ho Chi Minh in power in North Vietnam, let alone a potential leader of both sections, because he was a Communist. In general, Communists believed that the good of one's country was the most important goal, and they willingly sacrificed individual rights to achieve this goal. If the nation needed to raise more food, for example, whomever the government ordered into the fields had to go, even professionals such as doctors and lawyers. No one was allowed to criticize the government, and Communist leaders imprisoned—and sometimes executed—anyone who dared speak out against them. Although communism appalled most people who loved democracy, communism sometimes appealed to poor people, such as the many peasants in Vietnam, in large part because Communist leaders promised to take land and wealth away from the rich and share it with the poor.

Even though communism was seen as a threat as early as 1917 when the first successful Communist revolution took place in what became known as the Soviet Union, it wasn't until the end of World War II, when Communist-led governments took control of more and more countries, that Americans panicked. By late 1950, they were well aware that in addition to ruling the Soviet Union, Communists controlled eight countries in Eastern Europe as well as China and North Korea.

To make matters worse, powerful Communist leaders vowed to conquer the rest of the world. Therefore Americans saw themselves in mortal combat with Communists, and political leaders in the United States, driven by this fear, ruthlessly hunted down Communists at home and supported anti-Communist leaders abroad anyway they could. For example, the United States had helped finance France's war in Vietnam to try to prevent Ho Chi Minh's victory. American officials believed that if one more nation fell to communism, others would fall, too, like a row of dominoes, jeopardizing the entire free world.

Shortly after the meeting in Geneva ended, government officials in South Vietnam, who had no intention of holding an election they thought Ho Chi Minh would win, began to make preparations to defend their territory. These officials then asked the U.S. government for help.

America agreed to provide money and advice to help the South Vietnamese, believing that this would be all that was necessary to keep South Vietnam out of the clutches of the Communists. Most of the money and advice were used to establish an army for South Vietnam. The rest was earmarked for programs that were supposed to win the hearts and minds of the local citizens so that they would not support the Communists should elections ever take place. These programs included providing medical care for the poor and helping farmers raise better crops.

But the money and advice weren't effective for several reasons. First, the government of South Vietnam was very unpopular. Many South Vietnamese thought that government officials, especially Ngo Dinh Diem, were corrupt. These officials did little to help their reputations when they arrested anyone who questioned their policies, including religious leaders and war heroes who had fought valiantly against the French. Some of the South Vietnamese thought that Diem was not much better than Communists in this respect. Also, many South Vietnamese, well aware of America's support for the French, resented American advisors and any suggestions that they might make. As a result, no matter how many instructors the United States sent to Vietnam or how highly qualified they were, they were poorly received. In addition, the newly established South Vietnamese Army was not overly enthusiastic about supporting Diem.

Second, American aid failed in large part because of hard work done by Ho Chi Minh supporters who had entered South Vietnam when the country was divided. They went from village to village to help the poor and to try to convince them to vote for the Communists if elections should take place. They were so effective that support for the Communists grew rapidly in the countryside, and entire villages became supporters of Ho Chi Minh.

When South Vietnamese leaders refused to hold elections in 1956, various groups, most of which eventually united and were known as the Viet Cong, began to harass and even attack South Vietnamese troops and government officials to try to force a vote. American officials, driven by their fear of communism and ignoring the unpopularity of the South Vietnamese government, reacted by increasing their support for the South. President Dwight D. Eisenhower (1953–1961) promised to send more money and more advisors to Asia to show troops how to put down their opponents. Opponents of the South then sought aid from the North Vietnamese. Ho Chi Minh promised to send weapons, which would be transported over the Ho Chi Minh Trail. This long route crossed the highlands and meandered through the jungles all the way to the Mekong Delta. He also vowed to reunite the two sections. A major confrontation that would affect millions of lives in Asia and America was now in the making.

The Viet Cong's supplies and boldness increased in the next few years. Even so, President John F. Kennedy (1961–1963), the second of four presidents who led the United States during this very long

North and South Vietnam at the time of the Vietnam War

war, decided to limit American aid, as had President Eisenhower, to money and approximately fifteen thousand advisors.

Then, on August 2, 1964, North Vietnamese patrol boats fired on the U.S.S. *Maddox* in the Gulf of Tonkin. The North Vietnamese claimed that the boat was spying on their country. The third president to deal with the growing crisis, Lyndon B. Johnson (1963–1969), insisted that the *Maddox* was doing nothing of the sort. He called the shelling an unprovoked attack that demanded retaliation.

On August 4, President Johnson asked Congress for extraordinary power to deal with the crisis, which Congress granted. Shortly after, Johnson ordered the first of many bombing raids against North Vietnam to try to persuade Ho Chi Minh to stop supplying the Viet Cong with weapons. Johnson also promised the South Vietnamese more financial aid, more advisors, and for the first time, the support of American combat forces. These forces, in the form of 3,500 marines, arrived in March 1965. More soldiers were sent in the coming months, and by June 1965, American troops numbered 74,000. Polls conducted in the United States indicated that 80 percent of the American public supported Johnson's decision to send the troops.

The North Vietnamese responded by preparing for a long war. Ho Chi Minh, whose official title was "president," and his followers, including a growing number of South Vietnamese, planned to drive the latest invaders, the Americans, into the sea. The prime minister of North Vietnam, Pham Van Dong, who served as its main spokesman, made clear his country's determination to fight in an interview in early 1966. "How long do you Americans want to fight?" he asked. "One year? Two years? Three years? Five Years? Ten years? Twenty years? We will be glad to accommodate you."[3]

The United States responded with the best weapons available and overwhelming force, especially during the last years of President Johnson's term in office and the first years of Richard Nixon's presidency (1969–1974). Altogether, the United States spent $150 billion on the war effort and sent more than 2.5 million Americans to advise or fight. From 1965 to 1973, America dropped more bombs on the jungles and villages of Vietnam than it had on all of Europe in World

War II. The financial aid and number of troops made it possible for the United States and South Vietnam to win every major battle. But no matter how many losses the North Vietnamese and Viet Cong suffered, they simply refused to give up. They continued to fight until a war-weary America withdrew its forces, thereby enabling the North to win the conflict.

The costs of this loss, in addition to huge financial outlays, were enormous. More than 58,000 Americans died and 300,000 were wounded. Half of these suffered severe injuries that would affect them the rest of their lives. At least 1 million South Vietnamese died. Furthermore, instead of limiting the spread of communism, the war actually helped it gain new ground. Not only was all of Vietnam lost to communism, when the war spread to nearby Laos and Cambodia, the upheaval that resulted enabled the Communists there to take control in both countries. At least 1 million people—possibly as many as 2 million—died in these conflicts.

The victorious North Vietnamese, who sometimes resorted to using primitive weapons, such as sharp sticks dipped in poison, when they lacked money to buy guns, also suffered enormous losses. They buried more than 400,000 soldiers and 600,000 civilians, almost 10 percent of their population.

Americans did not know what was going on in Vietnam in the beginning of the war partly because of the lack of media coverage and partly because Americans were caught up in some dramatic battles of their own on the home front. These battles included the black community's civil-rights struggle, President Johnson's war on poverty, and a growing revolt among young people, especially college students, who actually seized control of some of America's universities to gain attention for their causes. These causes, which included having a greater voice in their education, would be replaced in the coming years with concerns about the war in Vietnam. The shocking assassinations of President Kennedy (1963), black leader Malcolm X (1965), civil-rights leader Martin Luther King, Jr. (1968), and presidential hopeful Robert Kennedy (1968), a brother of the slain president, further focused the public's attention on events at home.

It was also a time during which women were embroiled in a battle of their own. Some of them sought equality, a struggle that had begun almost two hundred years before. Part of this struggle involved a Constitutional amendment that had been drafted in 1923. The Equal Rights Amendment (ERA) stated that "men and women shall have equal rights throughout the United States and every place subject to its jurisdiction."[4] Although there had been a lot of enthusiasm for the amendment at first, it had failed to get enough support for ratification. Supporters now decided to revive the issue and eventually make the amendment the law of the land. The debate over equality became loud and contentious as it forced women to look at their lives and the roles that they were expected to play. More than a handful were disturbed by what they saw.

After World War II ended, many Americans simply wanted to lead quiet, comfortable lives surrounded by friends and family. This was especially true of returning soldiers. People married early and had, on average, two or more children. Men were expected to be the breadwinners, and women were expected to be stay-at-home moms and to run the household.

Because Americans had saved so much money during the war when wages were high and there were few consumer goods to purchase, many people could afford to buy homes when peace finally came. Construction of new houses soared, and almost one third of these were built in the suburbs, which was a new phenomenon.

All of these houses needed furnishings. War industries, which no longer could count on government orders for planes, ships, and guns, converted their plants. Now they made washing machines, clothes dryers, dishwashers, and the latest invention, television sets. Colorful ads in women's magazines were quite successful in convincing wives that their homes would be less than perfect without these appliances. As a result, the demand for the best and the latest goods was overwhelming.

The goals of early marriage, a comfortable home, and several children continued well into the 1960s. Many women in college then were more concerned with finding a potential husband than they

*A mother and her young daughter work in the kitchen in this
1953 photo. By the time the girl would become a mother herself,
the expectations society had for women, and women's expectations for
themselves, changed quite dramatically. The Vietnam War
helped bring about this change.*

were in passing their classes and starting a career. College women often talked about the three degrees available: the B.A. (Bachelor of Arts); the B.S. (Bachelor of Science); and the M.R.S (or "Mrs."). Women who were not engaged before graduation ceremonies were looked down upon. In some cases, they were even publicly humili-

*There were even fewer opportunities for black working women
in the United States after World War II. Often openly
discriminated against, 60 percent of black women who
worked during this time were maids.*

ated. For example, at the last breakfast of the school year held by
sorority members at the University of Missouri, any senior who was
not engaged had to eat a lemon in front of the group. This practice
continued until about 1962.

To attract a husband, women worked at making the best appearance possible. The image of what ladies should look like was rein-

forced by television programs of the day. Wives in popular programs, such as *Father Knows Best*, wore dresses, high heels, and pearls while cooking and cleaning.

At the same time, though, a number of women began to openly question their roles. Betty Friedan, a wife, mother, and writer, spoke for these women when she voiced "a strange stirring, a sense of dissatisfaction." She looked about and wondered, "Is this all?"[5]

For many like Friedan, running a household was not enough. While women's magazines were touting the good life at home, at least 30 percent of all women over the age of sixteen were working outside the home, either by choice or through necessity. However, many of these women were employed as waitresses, secretaries, or salesclerks. None of these positions paid well. If women could afford to attend college, they usually entered the nursing or teaching professions or became social workers or librarians, the few fields open to them. Many professional women were paid less than men who were doing comparable work. This upset working women, especially those who yearned for equality. Emboldened by the leaders of the civil-rights demonstrations and student protests, more and more women began to assert themselves.

So by the time the Vietnam War grabbed the public's attention, many women were no longer willing to be quiet observers. Some fought long and hard to serve in Vietnam; they faced danger every day 7,000 miles (11,265 kilometers) from home. Others fought equally hard to end America's participation in a war that they regarded as wrong to begin with and unwinnable to boot. This was an unpopular position for any American to take at the beginning of the war, let alone a woman. Protestors were called Communists, as well as a few other things, and for a while they encountered public condemnation and risked brutal attacks for their beliefs. Both positions required enormous courage, and although these women, supporters and protesters alike, would not have called themselves special, they were anything but ordinary. They were the valiant women of the Vietnam War.

Except for nurses in Korea [1950–1953], U.S. women had not served in a combat theater since World War II [1941–1945], and there were strong sentiments in some circles that they did not belong in Vietnam.

MAJOR GENERAL JEANNE HOLM

2 IN THE ARMED FORCES

American women have served in the armed forces at every opportunity in the nation's history. However, in the early years, when the very thought of a woman on a battlefield was enough to cause the average person to gasp, the first female soldiers assumed men's names and enlisted in disguise. Deborah Sampson, who fought in the Revolutionary War (1775–1783), was one of the country's first known female warriors. How many served with her is not certain, but historians know that she was not the only woman on the battlefield during America's long fight for independence from England. During the Civil War (1861–1865), about four hundred women fought, again in men's clothing, and at least one became an officer.

In the 1900s, women fought for the right to serve their country in wartime without having to pretend that they were men. Besides, physical exams were now required before one could join the armed services, making it almost impossible for females to enlist as males. During America's participation in World War I (1917–1918), women clamored for the right to serve. But it wasn't until the armed forces were strapped for manpower toward the end of the war that they agreed to accept a few women whose tasks would be limited to support services. At the end of the war, women were among the first to be relieved of their duties.

When World War II broke out, women again struggled to serve their country. In 1941, Edith Nourse Rogers, congresswoman from Massachusetts, introduced a bill in the House of Representatives to form the Women's Army Auxiliary Corps, whose members eventually became known as WACs. Even though women's participation would be limited to noncombat positions, the bill was so controversial that ninety-six representatives and thirty-one senators refused to vote on it. Some congressmen wondered aloud about who would do the cooking, washing, and mending at home if women went into the army. One representative thought that the presence of women in the services was humiliating. What, he wanted to know, had happened to the manhood of America? Couldn't men win wars without the help of ladies? The bill became law despite strong opposition, and shortly after, all branches of the armed services—including the army, the air force, the navy, and the marines—began to accept female volunteers.

But accepting women for training was just the first part of the struggle. So many military leaders believed that women were emotionally and physically unfit for the rigors of war that they refused to work with female recruits. Some admirals even said that they preferred to have dogs, ducks, or even monkeys on their staff rather than women. Even so, some military leaders were willing to take a chance on women, and by the end of the war, 300,000 had served as typists, truck drivers, air-traffic controllers, mechanics, and much more.

Even the most reluctant soldiers had to admit that the women had proved themselves to be more than capable of handling wartime duties. General Dwight D. Eisenhower, who worked with WACs in Africa and Europe, spoke for many when he said, "When this project was proposed . . . like most old soldiers, I was violently against it. . . .

Every phase of the record they compiled during the war convinced me of the error of my first reaction. . . . They were a model for the Army."[1]

In fact, women in the military had done so well during World War II that they became a permanent part of the armed services in 1948. This did not mean that they were equal to male soldiers, though. First of all, since a strong combat force was thought necessary and women were not allowed to fight, only 2 percent of the total number of military personnel, about 30,000, could be female. These volunteers were kept in separate units: the WACs, WAVEs, Women Marines, and WAFs, who worked with the newly established air force. Also, women could now have careers in the military. However, they could not hope to achieve the promotions that male officers might receive, such as the rank of general, for example.

Although there were some highly skilled career women in the services in the years leading up to the Vietnam War, some of whom had served in World War II, new recruits, reflecting society at the time, were chosen more for their appearance than their abilities. One high-ranking WAC officer sneered when she referred to the selection of volunteers as a "beauty contest." Basic training no longer included extensive physical-fitness programs or even an introduction to weapons. Instead, the women took classes on posture, makeup, and styling one's hair. They were expected to match their lipstick and nail polish to the trim on their uniforms and to wear high heels, white gloves, and hats. The emphasis on appearance led one WAC to comment that she had "known Campfire Girls more rugged than we are!"[2] As a result of their lack of rigorous training, it wasn't surprising that few military leaders thought about sending women to Vietnam.

But the lack of training, which could easily be changed, wasn't the only excuse the military used to limit women's roles in Vietnam. This war, military leaders pointed out, was very different from other wars. In the past, fighting had taken place on battlefronts, and women were assigned to sites behind these lines where they were relatively safe. However, in South Vietnam there was no front. Because American women had not proved that they could function in a guer-

An off-duty woman marine interacts with some Vietnamese children in Saigon in 1968.

rilla war (and, of course, couldn't until given a chance to do so), many military leaders were reluctant to send them to Asia even when the women asked to go.

Women in the military, especially those who were career-minded, considered the government's refusal to honor their request a slap in the face. They argued that female volunteers, such as Red Cross workers, for example, were in South Vietnam, and they were managing quite well. So were nuns and other women from various religious organizations. WACs, WAVEs, WAFs, and Women Marines alike pointed out that the skills of five support staff members were needed for each soldier in the field, who could hardly order his own food, make arrangements for shelter and uniforms, or type out his orders and records himself. More important, most members of the support staff, males, were being trained for jobs that even the newest female recruits could do: typing, filing, and answering telephones.

When military leaders refused to budge, several women publicly voiced their anger. A WAC lieutenant said, "There's a war going on in Vietnam, but you have to be a civilian to be assigned there. Women are fighting in the jungles with the Viet Cong, but we aren't allowed to dirty our dainty hands!"[3] Another, a master sergeant who had served in World War II, said, "I served in North Africa and Italy—and I can sure as hell serve in Vietnam."[4]

When women in the U.S. military learned that two WACs, Major Kathleen I. Wilkes and Master Sergeant Betty Adams, had been sent to Vietnam in January 1965 to help the South Vietnamese set up a training program for Vietnamese volunteers for the Women's Armed Forces Corps, they became even more adamant about going to Asia. Why, they wondered aloud, was it safe for some WACs to serve in the conflict and not others?

Besides wanting to serve their country and prove that women could function well in any kind of war, career women looked upon the military's refusal to send them to Asia as a serious obstacle to their advancement. Men who served in Vietnam, a one-year tour, received extra pay and were allowed to pick their next assignment. In addition, they were given more training, and were promised accelerated promotions. So shortly after the first marines arrived in Vietnam in 1965, leaders of the women's military organizations began a determined effort to get large numbers of women in the armed forces assigned to Asia. They were only partially successful.

The break that the women were waiting for came in the fall of 1965. General William Westmoreland, a veteran of three wars and commander of American forces in Vietnam, had become deeply concerned about the paperwork that was piling up in the military headquarters in Saigon. Because this paperwork was expected to increase over the coming months and women were begging for an opportunity to serve in Asia, Westmoreland decided to request help from the WACs, who were under the command of Colonel Elizabeth P. Hoisington. Only a few were sent at first, and then only to Saigon, the headquarters of the American forces, which was thought to be a relatively safe post.

Few historians can agree on how many women in the armed forces served in Vietnam, since military records are incomplete. Some sources claim that 7,500 military women were in South Vietnam; others think that the actual number is closer to 11,000. In either case, the vast majority of these women were nurses. However, records also show that at least 500 WACs, and perhaps as many as 600, worked in the military headquarters in Saigon or at the new army base at Long Binh. The air force assigned 600 WAFs, half of whom were officers, all of whom were support staff, to Vietnam. The Women Marines sent 36 women. The navy, which played a smaller role in Vietnam than the other services did, needed fewer support workers and therefore assigned few WAVEs to Asia. Actually, there probably were never more than three WAVEs in Vietnam at any one time, in spite of the fact that women in the navy repeatedly asked to serve in the war.

Ironically, even though the armed services thought that women's abilities were limited, especially in this war, government officials decided to try to recruit more women. This decision was due to the

Vietnamese Women at War

While American women were struggling for the right to participate in the war in Vietnam, many Vietnamese women were already deeply involved in the conflict. Official records show that thousands of South Vietnamese women—at least 3,000 in 1966 alone—served as support staff for the South Vietnamese Army after being trained by American WACs. At the same time, others served unofficially, carrying messages and gathering information. And some fought with the army. One woman warrior, Ho Te Que, the mother of seven children, was called the "Tiger Lady of the Delta." She led South Vietnamese soldiers to Viet Cong hideouts until her death on the battlefield in 1965.

At the same time, many women served in Viet Cong units, making up one fourth to almost half of the total number of soldiers in some units. These women transported weapons on the Ho Chi Minh Trail, fired antiaircraft guns, and spied for the North. Some eventually formed guerrilla bands of their own, and a number of these women became noted for their superior marksmanship.

Vietnamese girls learn to use rifles in a secret clearing in a South Vietnamese forest in September 1967.

fact that the current draft law, which required all physically able men to register on their eighteenth birthdays and to serve in the armed services if called, would expire in 1967.

Fearing that Congress might decide to have an all-volunteer armed forces, which would most likely reduce the number of recruits at the very time that the United States was planning to increase its personnel in South Vietnam, government officials decided to remove the 2 percent quota on women. Instead of limiting their numbers to 30,000, government officials aimed for 36,500 in 1968 and a whopping total of 180,000 by 1977. To get more volunteers, officials promised more educational opportunities, and they made it possible for women to achieve the highest ranks, including that of general. These women not only could provide support services, they could free men for combat if necessary.

The jobs that military women performed in Vietnam varied greatly, depending upon their rank and training. Most WACs, like Linda J. McClenahan, worked in the army's communications center at Long Binh, and they processed stacks upon stacks of vital information. Details about troop movements and surveillance reports about the enemy's activities were sent to Long Binh, sorted, and then passed on to the appropriate officers. Casualty reports were also sent to this site. When a soldier was wounded or killed, McClenahan prepared a report for the soldier's branch of service as well as the fort nearest the soldier's home so that his family could be notified.

Other WACs, such as Pinkie Houser, worked in highly classified areas. Houser served with thirty officers who were in charge of all the electrical power and bridges in South Vietnam. Houser, who had top-secret clearance, kept records for this group.

Even though military officers tried to assign women to supposedly safe spots, some of the women had to leave their bases in order to perform their jobs. Houser was one of these women. Sometimes she accompanied her supervisors when they checked bridges and power lines, usually from a helicopter. When she did so, she traded her dress uniform and heels for green fatigues and a pair of boots, as did many women in Vietnam. She also donned a bulletproof vest and packed a sidearm, which she had recently been trained to use.

Other WACs in Saigon and Long Binh used their skills to decode messages, order supplies, and coordinate the schedules of incoming dignitaries and diplomats. A few acted as escorts for these dignitaries, keeping them out of harm's way as much as possible.

Like the WACs, women in the air force also performed a variety of jobs. Major Norma Archer gave air-strike briefings each day. She narrated films shot the previous day during combat as well as clips of possible sightings of the Viet Cong. She was the first WAF in history to give such briefings. She also coordinated still pictures, supervised photo development, and organized film libraries for sixteen units in Vietnam.

While Archer was coordinating the information that came in, other WAFs were helping photographers film the war. The armed services were not eager to have reporters wandering about on their own in Vietnam, fearing that they might run into the Viet Cong. To protect them, reporters were teamed with an information officer who escorted them in the field and provided the latest facts about the conflict.

When WAF information officers first volunteered to go to Vietnam, several military leaders refused to accept the women's help. Information officers, the naysayers said, had to perform escort duty at any hour, day or night, to any point in Vietnam. They would be required to fly on combat aircraft and even provide physical assistance for the newsmen, such as carrying camera equipment and recorders. This was just too much to expect from women.

Brigadier General Robert Dixon, after studying the women's records, rose to their defense. He said that they had the skills to be first-rate information officers. Furthermore, he added, he remembered seeing women reporters carrying cameras and recorders, working at all hours, and flying on combat aircraft as well. If reporters could do this, he wondered aloud, why couldn't female officers do the same? Dixon's support was all that was needed. The first WAF information officers arrived in Vietnam in the fall of 1967.

Unlike the WAFs, Women Marines served in very small numbers, usually eight to ten enlisted women and one or two officers at a time.

Major General Jeanne Holm, USAF

Major general Jeanne Holm at the time of her promotion to General in 1971

In 1971, Major General Jeanne Holm became the first woman general in the United States Air Force and the highest-ranking woman in the entire armed services. Holm began her military career in 1942, when she joined the WACs as a truck driver. By the end of World War II, she had been promoted to captain. Like many women in the military then, she left the armed services at the end of the war.

In 1948 she was recalled to duty. Holm was then transferred to the air force. She was uncertain about making the service her career, "but," she said, "the Air Force kept sending me to interesting places and giving me good jobs."[5]

Once American servicemen were assigned to Vietnam, Holm asked to have WAFs assigned to the combat zone as support staff. When her request was denied, she flew to Asia to personally present her case to her superiors. Shortly after, Lieutenant Colonel June H. Hilton and five enlisted WAFs arrived in Saigon. Holm then turned her attention to providing a greater variety of assignments for women in the war zone, a task that took a little longer to complete.

Even after her retirement in 1975, General Holm continued to work on behalf of women in the military. She was a member of the Defense Advisory Committee on Women in the Services for three years, and she wrote a book, *Women in the Military: An Unfinished Revolution*, in which she presented a strong case for having women in the military and an equally strong case for making changes in the armed services that would make it possible for these women to excel.

The first of these women to serve was Master Sergeant Barbara J. Dulinsky, who arrived in Saigon in March 1967. Most of the Women Marines performed administrative tasks in various headquarters throughout Vietnam. Some of the women were historians. They recorded battle information for posterity.

Almost all of the military women in Vietnam worked twelve hours a day, six days a week. They endured shellings and spent many hours in bunkers, waiting for the enemy to attack. In addition, many military units adopted either a hospital or a local orphanage. Whenever possible, the women spent their days off visiting wounded soldiers or distributing clothing sent from the United States to Vietnamese children.

Even so, many of these women still felt that they weren't doing enough to win the war, and this haunted them, especially after South Vietnam and the United States lost the conflict. Fifteen years after she served in Vietnam, Linda McClenahan said, "I have finally accepted the fact that . . . I couldn't have done anything more than what I did to help those people. . . . I couldn't have done anything to change the fact that people died . . . people that I knew and cared about and loved, and strangers too . . . and for such a long time I kept thinking that I should have been able to do more."[6]

Martha Raye, who was a famous comedian and a frequent entertainer at military shows in Vietnam during the war, met many of the American women in Asia. She saw how hard they worked to support the war effort, and she doubted that more could have been done. She said, "I think it's important that [Americans] know that women did their share, more than their share, if that's possible. Our country owes them profound thanks."[7]

*[During an attack, nurses] had to go around
[hospitals] dragging guys off the beds and getting
them under the beds or bringing the mattresses up
and covering them. . . . If the attack was bad, we
would lower the operating tables . . . so we could
operate on our knees.*

LYNDA VAN DEVANTER, U.S. ARMY NURSE

CARING FOR 3
THE WOUNDED

American women were first allowed to serve as combat nurses during
the Civil War. At that time, the North and South were so poorly prepared for battle that both sections had to ask citizens to help treat
the wounds of injured soldiers and nurse them back to health. Even
though women's roles were very limited then, nursing on a volunteer
basis was acceptable because it was seen as an extension of women's
work, part of which was caring for sick family members, friends, and
neighbors.

The volunteers did so well that government officials, desperately
short of male nurses, decided to take women into the nursing corps.
To make sure that there would be no "scandalous" behavior between
nurses and patients, which was a real concern at that time, women
who applied for work had to be plain and considerably older than the
soldiers they would treat. Applicants also had to have at least one

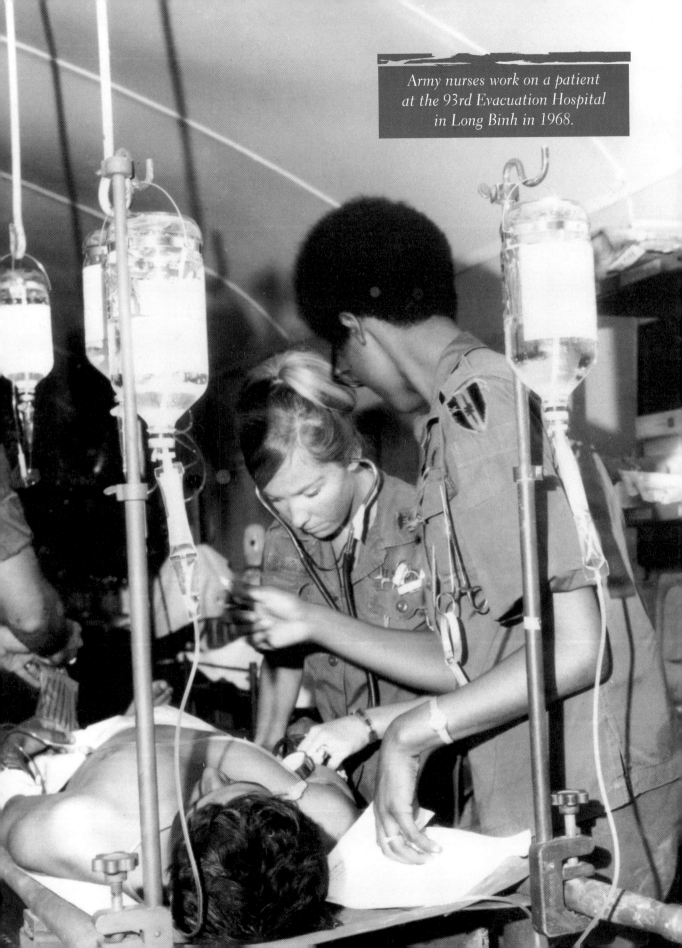

character reference, preferably from their pastor or priest, to prove that they were of the highest moral caliber.

These nurses proved beyond any doubt that they could perform their duties under great stress, even when they were close to enemy fire. Actually, they did so well that when the next wars broke out, no one objected to sending female nurses to the front. In fact, during World War II, when it appeared that a nursing shortage was in sight, several congressmen even talked about drafting women for the nursing corps.

When American troops were sent to Vietnam, armed forces recruiters visited nursing schools seeking volunteers for the army, navy, and air force nursing corps. Nursing students who agreed to serve for three years after they received their license were given a monthly payment that would cover living expenses and tuition. This was especially appealing to women from poor families who often found that working to pay their tuition costs while going to school was difficult at best.

About seven thousand women served as nurses in Vietnam. The vast majority of these women were in the army, and they worked in one of seven surgical facilities, ten field hospitals (which were similar to American hospitals), or eleven evacuation centers, sites from which seriously wounded soldiers were sent to other hospitals, either in Asia or America. Because there were so many medical facilities and an abundance of helicopters, few soldiers were more than ten minutes away from medical help. This meant that more injured men would survive. It also meant that doctors and nurses treated horrendous wounds that, had they been received in other wars, would have resulted in death before the injured reached a medical center.

Few nurses were prepared for the horrors that they saw. Ruth Sidisin, who was an experienced nurse, said, "Not even working with earthquake victims or in the emergency room of a big hospital could equal what I saw in a single day in Vietnam. . . . There were belly wounds, amputations, head injuries, burns. On top of that they all had infections and complications. They had things we'd never heard about in school—things some of the physicians had never even heard about—and diseases they told us people hardly ever got anymore. Dengue fever. Malaria. Hepatitis. Bubonic plague."[1]

Treating such wounds was difficult enough with only a few patients, but in January 1968 the numbers of wounded suddenly sky-rocketed, overwhelming medical teams. Ignoring a truce and a highly celebrated Vietnamese holiday—the Lunar New Year, or Tet—70,000 North Vietnamese and about 200,000 Viet Cong struck without warning. During this assault, known as the Tet offensive, these troops attacked thirty-six provincial capitals in South Vietnam and seventy-two small towns. The Communists also shelled American military bases all across the South, all at the same time. Stunned South Vietnamese troops, 600,000 strong, and 500,000 American soldiers were so unprepared that the enemy was actually able to enter Saigon and seize the American embassy for a while. Although the Communists eventually were forced to flee, they inflicted enormous casualties before they sought refuge. This attack was the first of such magnitude, and it harshly tested the skills of military doctors and nurses.

During such emergencies, medical teams used a system known as "triage." After a quick examination, the teams made life-and-death choices. They divided the wounded into three groups: expectants, soldiers who would not survive, even with the best medical care; men who might survive; and those who would most likely live. Expectants were placed in a separate area and made as comfortable as possible. The others were treated very quickly, starting with those who needed the least care, in order to help many patients as quickly as possible. In the case of multiple wounds, several surgical teams worked on one victim at the same time. One team might treat a soldier's head injuries while the second removed a shattered leg or arm.

Although a typical nursing shift was twelve hours long, during emergencies such as the Tet offensive, it was not unusual for nurses to work thirty hours before collapsing from exhaustion. Army nurses also provided medical care for Vietnamese civilians, especially children, and Communist prisoners of war.

In a guerrilla war, everyone and everything is a fair target, even a hospital. When one was hit, nurses had to protect their patients as best they could. Patients were given helmets to wear, placed beneath beds if possible, or, if they couldn't be moved, covered with mattresses. If the electricity went out, nurses checked on their patients with flashlights and ran emergency generators to keep lifesaving equipment, such as respirators, operating. Often the nurses' most difficult task was trying to calm the soldiers, who sometimes cried out for a weapon so that they could fight back.

Attacks on hospitals killed patients, medics, doctors, and nurses alike. The first nurse to die as a result of enemy fire in Vietnam was twenty-five-year-old Army Lieutenant Sharon Lane. On June 8, 1969, at 5:55 A.M., she was about to awaken her patients in a hospital in Chu Lai when it was attacked by the Viet Cong. A rocket exploded near her, and she was killed instantly. Seven more nurses would die before the war ended.

Air force nurses worked in evacuation hospitals. They stabilized patients for their flight to American hospitals located on U.S. military bases in Japan, the Philippines, or the United States for specialized medical care, or treated patients during the flights. In either case, workdays were at least twelve hours long, and often the nurses were dealing with some of the most seriously wounded soldiers. This kept the nurses on edge. First Lieutenant Margaret LaBarbera, a nurse in the emergency room of the 71st Evacuation Hospital in Pleiku, said, "I just don't know what will be coming in, so I just pray that the injured will make it and . . . put my full effort into making things ready for their arrival."[2]

In addition to administering traditional medical care, flight nurses had to be prepared to treat the special problems that flying presented. Some of the planes used for transporting patients were former cargo carriers. These carriers could land on dirt runways, and they could make steep climbs or descents, which was very important when the enemy was shooting at the plane. However, cargo planes were not heavily pressurized. The change in air pressure as the plane reached high altitudes caused physical changes in patients. For example, oxygen in the bloodstream expanded, sometimes causing new wounds to rupture. Therefore, nurses had to constantly monitor their patients. Flight nurses also had to keep the medical equipment in place and functioning as a plane took off or landed at as many as

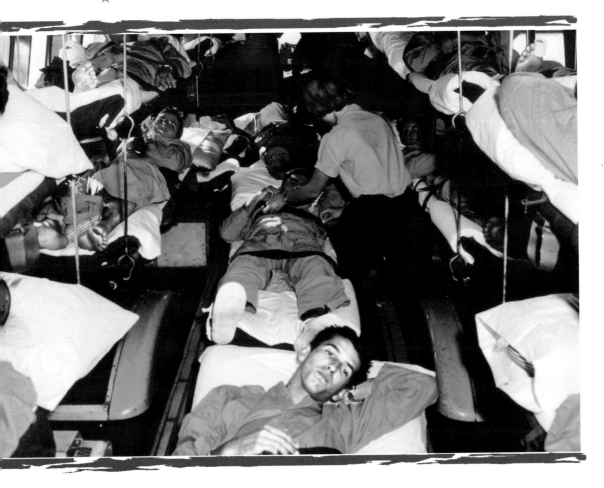

U.S. Air Force 2nd Lieutenant Patricia Hines checks the safety belts of patients aboard an ambulance bus taking wounded servicemen to an aircraft for evacuation to Japan in 1968.

ten different sites each day, crisscrossing Vietnam to pick up more and more patients for a distant destination.

Like army nurses, air force nurses came under fire. Sometimes their planes took off before the doors were closed. One nurse said, "We had to get in the air because they were shooting at us."[3]

Most nurses in the navy served aboard hospital ships. The first floating hospital, the U.S.S. *Repose* was ready for patients in October

1965, just before the bombing of North Vietnam began. Twenty-nine nurses were assigned to this ship. At first the *Repose* was located just off the coast of Vietnam. But when Viet Cong divers tried to tie a bomb to the ship's anchor, naval officials decided to move the ship out to sea. One year later, the U.S.S. *Sanctuary*, again with twenty-nine nurses, joined the *Repose*.

Nurses aboard these ships were expected to be on duty for thirty days at a time. But sometimes there were so many injured sailors to care for that nurses worked for more than one hundred days without a break. These women were experts at administering medications when the ship was tossed about in a typhoon, and at lashing down every piece of equipment to keep it from rolling around.

Some of the navy nurses, such as Maureen Walsh, served at naval bases. One of Walsh's jobs was to help train corpsmen, who assisted nurses and doctors in the hospitals. Like many medical teams, Walsh's unit was always improving its procedures for treating patients. During the war, she helped design a shock-trauma setup for the navy's Intensive Care Unit, to be used in conjunction with helicopter rescue teams. This model was so successful that it was copied by trauma units in the United States after the war. In 1985, Walsh was seriously injured in an automobile accident in Maryland. She was treated in the same kind of trauma unit that she had helped to design, which she credited for saving her life.[4]

Although their work was dangerous and incredibly demanding, most nurses who served in Vietnam regarded their time there as the most challenging and most satisfying year of their careers. One spoke for many when she said, "I'm not sure I've ever enjoyed nursing as much as I did that year. It was the most exciting, the most challenging, the most stressful, and the most important nursing practice I've ever done."[5]

And their work did not go unnoticed. Anne Allen, a reporter in Vietnam during the war, said, "One thing I want to say—those medics and those nurses performed feats that I can't describe in any other way than to say they were heroic."[6] Their patients would have agreed.

When I first made up my mind to go over to Nam . . .
I was a volunteer hostess at the USO airport lounge,
dealing with the Vietnam vets as they were going over
or coming home from Vietnam. I always wanted to
be part of this war. I wanted to help. I just wanted to
be able to show the [soldiers] that somebody really cared.

MAUREEN NERLI, USO VOLUNTEER

4 MORE VOLUNTEERS IN VIETNAM

The total number of women who agreed to risk their lives by serving in Vietnam varies from source to source. The smallest estimate is 33,000 (including all military women, nurses, and support staff); the highest is 55,000. Most of the women who were not in the military or nursing corps were volunteers who were hired by the armed services to help soldiers or employed by relief organizations such as the Red Cross.

During World War II, several religious groups started the United Service Organizations (USO). This organization established sites near military bases, mostly in the United States, where soldiers could meet friends, play a game of cards, or socialize with local young women. These centers were run by volunteer hostesses who had been screened carefully and given lessons on how to conduct themselves politely and cheerfully at all times.

Debra Barnes, Miss America 1968, talks with soldiers after a USO show in which she performed.

The USO was so well received that it continued to operate after the war ended. The number of sites expanded over the years, and came to include lounges at major airports that soldiers were likely to pass through, and provided many homes away from home for soldiers in times of peace as well as during times of conflict.

When American soldiers were sent to Vietnam, twenty-five USO sites were established in the South. The USO then hired and trained hundreds of American women, all civilians, who volunteered to go overseas to staff these sites. Most volunteers served for eighteen months.

Maureen Nerli was one of these volunteers. She was an associate director of a USO club in Tan Son Nhut. Her club, she later recalled, "was a four-story building. . . . We had pool and Ping-Pong tables, overseas telephones, a barber shop, and gift shop. We served between five hundred and eight hundred shakes, hot dogs, and hamburgers every day. . . . The [soldiers] came from all over Vietnam—Tan Son Nhut, Long Binh, Da Nang—you name it."[1]

Nerli's job also included visiting nearby bases. Although she and other staff members organized special celebrations, such as Irish Day or Octoberfest, they also put a lot of effort into providing entertainment for the soldiers. The USO hired singers, dancers, and bands from the United States to entertain the soldiers. When entertainers weren't available, the women drafted soldiers to form bands, lead sing-a-longs, and model in fashion shows.

Army Special Services also hired volunteers to provide similar entertainment for the troops in Vietnam. In addition, Special Services coordinated tours of movie stars who volunteered to give shows for the soldiers.

Most volunteers lived on or near army bases, which put them in danger. Judy Jenkins, who worked for Special Services, described one threat in a letter to a friend. She said, "Last month [January 1968, the Tet offensive] there were the worst attacks ever all over Vietnam. . . . We were all scared. Military intelligence reported that our base might be in danger of being overrun from a [North Vietnamese Army] battalion in our area. We lived in underground bunkers for several days, but the major attack never came. We only had a few rockets and a small sniper attack." [2]

Employees of the Red Cross in Vietnam worked closely with the armed services to provide support for the soldiers. Staff members, who ran 28 sites in Vietnam, some for as long as 10 years, arranged emergency loans, relayed messages between soldiers and their families, and manned the Supplemental Recreational Activities Overseas (SRAO) program, an entertainment program similar to those of the USO and Special Services. At least 1,100 women worked with the Red Cross in Vietnam, and almost half of them were employed by the SRAO. These volunteers served for one year.

During World War II, SRAO women were called "donut dollies," because they distributed so many donuts and cups of hot coffee to soldiers. Although some of the Red Cross workers in Vietnam were called donut dollies as well, another name, "chopper chicks," was also used, because the women were routinely transported by helicopters when they visited bases and units in the field.

Jeanne Christie was a chopper chick. She worked in Nha Trang and Da Nang. Typically, her day began when she arrived at the airport at dawn. She and her partner would then be flown to six or eight units in the field each day. Their arrival always got attention. Christie said, "The guys would sit on the hill or whatever and watch us in total awe. Some of them would flock to you and talk as fast as they could; others couldn't say a thing. But all of them would stare. They knew every movement we made—nothing we did escaped them."[3] After visiting with the men, Christie and her partner would lead the soldiers in audience-participation games such as Concentration. The sillier the game was, the more the men liked it. The goal was to laugh and forget the dangers of war, at least for the duration of the program. If time permitted, the women ate a meal with the men or handed out cups of Kool-Aid.

SRAO staffers also visited wounded soldiers in the hospitals. Unlike providing entertainment and making the men laugh, which was fun, this part of the job was traumatic. "We were not prepared," SRAO staffer Penni Evans recalled. "Not that any of the nurses or

A unit of Donut Dollies poses in front of a chopper in 1970.

others in the medical profession were prepared for what happens in a war, but we had no training whatsoever . . . . You would go into the hospital and walk through the wards of torn up, mutilated bodies. . . . What do you say?"[4]

Because the fighting situation changed rapidly in Vietnam, volunteers in the field were always at risk. Some programs were cut short—fast—when the enemy was spotted in the area. The women were then put aboard helicopters and flown to their next assignment. Considering the risk they took, it's amazing that only five Red Cross workers died in Vietnam, and none of these deaths was the result of enemy fire.

While the workers involved with the USO, Army Special Services, and the Red Cross concentrated on supporting and helping American soldiers in Vietnam, another large group of volunteers went to Vietnam to help the Vietnamese people. These workers, members of various relief groups, did not take sides, at least in the beginning of the war. But as the war dragged on, even some of the most determinedly neutral volunteers, sickened and dismayed at the rising number of deaths and the victimization of helpless civilians, found it impossible to remain aloof or even to remain in Vietnam.

Some volunteers worked for USAID, an organization funded by the U.S. government. USAID workers included nurses and doctors to treat civilians, and agricultural specialists to help peasants replant their fields when their crops had been destroyed. Volunteers also worked at orphanages to help care for the growing number of orphaned children—nearly 800,000 by the end of the war.[5]

Other volunteers, like Marjorie Nelson, worked for religious organizations. Nelson was a member of the American Friends Service Committee, a Quaker organization dedicated to helping people who have been victimized by war. Marjorie was assigned to a rehabilitation center in Quang Ngai. This center specialized in helping amputees, many of whom had been victimized by land mines. The center also provided medical help to napalm victims. Napalm, a jellylike chemical dropped from planes, stripped trees and underbrush of their leaves, and it was used by American forces to expose the Viet

Red Cross on the Home Front

While some Red Cross volunteers worked in Vietnam, others were busy on the home front. These workers, many of whom were women, relayed messages between soldiers and their loved ones, organized massive blood drives, and packed more than 3 million "ditty bags," sacks that contained items such as toothpaste, soap, candy, and gum for the soldiers in Asia.

Red Cross volunteers also organized a major campaign to force the North Vietnamese to treat American prisoners of war in a more humane fashion. The Communists insisted that their captives, especially pilots who had bombed North Vietnam, were "war criminals" and therefore not eligible for the kind of treatment that prisoners of war had the right to expect. Furthermore, the Communists would not allow Red Cross workers to visit the prison camps to talk to the men and see how they were being treated.

When the Vietnamese paraded prisoners through the streets of Hanoi and photographs of the men reached the United States, Americans were outraged. The soldiers were clearly not receiving proper care. The Red Cross responded by leading a "Write Hanoi" campaign in 1969 to put pressure on the Communists to treat their captives better. Deluged by letters and put in the international spotlight, the North Vietnamese finally agreed to let the men receive food packages from the Red Cross in 1970. When the letters continued to pour in, the Communists even agreed to let Red Cross workers inspect some of the camps in 1971.

Cong in the dense tropical jungle. This chemical also burned flesh as fast as it scorched leaves, and because it didn't differentiate between soldiers and civilians, anyone who was in the area was severely burned.

After months of hard work, Nelson left the center to visit Hue, in the northern part of South Vietnam, just before the Tet offensive took place in 1968. When the surprise attack began and North Vietnamese soldiers overran the city, she was staying with her friend Sandy Johnson, an American teacher of English. As soon as the shelling started, they took refuge in a hastily constructed shelter made from sandbags and Johnson's dining room table. They spent two nights and a day beneath this table, wondering if they would survive. When soldiers who had a list of the residences of all foreigners in the city pounded on the door, the women acted as if no one was home. The men responded by tossing a grenade at the front of the house.

The soldiers eventually returned and took Nelson and Johnson into custody. The women were taken to the mountains to a prisoner-of-war (POW) camp, where they were held for two months in a little house made of branches and bamboo stalks. Once the North Vietnamese were convinced that neither woman was associated with the U.S. armed forces and the women promised to leave Vietnam if released, they were given their freedom.

Sandra Collingwood was also in Hue when the North Vietnamese attacked. She worked for International Voluntary Services (IVS), which, like USAID and the Friends Committee, tried to help Vietnamese civilians who had been hurt by the war. Collingwood's specialty was community development, and when she learned that a nearby fishing village had been nearly destroyed during the Tet offensive, she volunteered to help the villagers rebuild. But her supervisors refused to send her there, arguing that the Viet Cong were simply too active in the area. She later said, "I knew that area, and I felt I could be helpful. This is something that was a common theme that ran through the whole time I was there . . . that I would not be able to go to an area because I was a woman or an American."[6]

A Red Cross recreation worker checks a soldier's blindfold during a game she conducted at a base near the front line in Vietnam.

Deeply discouraged, Collingwood eventually left IVS and joined yet another relief organization, Catholic Relief Services. But even though she was now allowed to work more closely with the Vietnamese, the continuing destruction dismayed and finally overwhelmed her. She saw no reason to help the peasants rebuild their villages or replant their fields only to have them demolished again and again during search-and-destroy raids by American and South Vietnamese forces or savage attacks by the North Vietnamese. The only way to help these people, she decided, was to end the war, and in her opinion, that meant withdrawing American forces. "I had by this time [1969]," she said, "reached a very strong opinion that none of us foreigners should be there, whether we were carrying guns or not. I felt if anything was going to be done as far as ending the war . . . it was by convincing our government at home that we needed to pull out of Vietnam."[7]

Shortly after, Collingwood left Asia. She would be followed by many other disheartened volunteers in the coming months.

I recognized the danger of [Vietnam], the risk of it, but still . . . it appealed to me."

ETHEL L. PAYNE, JOURNALIST

5 WAR CORRESPONDENTS

Women were first granted the right to be war correspondents in World War I. But it took so long to persuade the armed services to allow women to get close to the battlefront, that by the time they were given permission to go, the war was over.

When American soldiers were sent to Europe and Asia in World War II, female journalists in the United States once again pleaded for the right to cover the story. The heated debates that followed were won by the women, and within months after America entered the war, they were writing about the American soldiers' valiant struggle to defeat the enemy.

More than one of these women made headlines during the war, sometimes outwitting and outmaneuvering their male colleagues to be the first to file a story. Marguerite Higgins and Martha Gellhorn, for example, were so successful that they continued to work as war correspondents after World War II ended, covering conflicts all over the world.

Although American journalists have had a great deal of freedom while reporting the news, freedom of the press has sometimes been limited during wartime. When World War I was raging across Europe, Congress passed legislation that made it illegal for Americans to criticize their government during the conflict. Most Americans willingly accepted this, believing that it was important for the country to appear united during such a crisis. During World War II, the media, which included newspapers, magazines, radio broadcasts, and newsreels shown at movie theaters, censored themselves, making sure that they did not intentionally say anything that would help or encourage the enemy. The media also refused to show the American public the realities and horrors of the war. Instead, editors selected their words and pictures very carefully, as they did during the next war, the Korean Conflict.

In the beginning of the Vietnam War, the media, which now included television journalists, supported America's limited role in the conflict. Information officers worked closely with reporters, the first of whom arrived in 1960—four years after the first American advisors were sent to Vietnam. Officers gave reports to correspondents each day, citing impressive statistics to prove that the South Vietnamese troops were making progress against the Viet Cong during search-and-destroy raids. Somehow South Vietnamese soldiers and American advisors had determined how many Viet Cong were supposedly active in South Vietnam. When this number was reached, the South Vietnamese would no longer be at risk.

In December 1962, South Vietnamese troops received word about a Viet Cong stronghold near Ap Bac. In January 1963, the South Vietnamese, who outnumbered their opponents ten to one, closed in on this stronghold. The Viet Cong dug in for a long fight, putting up a resistance that stunned the South Vietnamese before they slipped through their enemy's lines to safety. American advisors called it a great triumph because the enemy had been driven out, but correspondents questioned the advisors' conclusions. Hadn't the goal been to capture the Viet Cong? reporters asked. The doubt created by the advisors' comments created skepticism, and soon many correspondents were questioning almost all of the information provided by government officials.

Shortly after the battle at Ap Bac and two years before American troops arrived in Vietnam, Marguerite Higgins prepared to go to Asia. She already had quite a reputation as a war correspondent. At the end of World War II, Higgins was one of the first reporters to enter a concentration camp in Germany, where thousands of Jews had been killed. In 1950, she went to Korea. Her vivid accounts of the heroic efforts of American soldiers there won the Pulitzer Prize for foreign correspondence in 1951. She was the first woman to receive this award.

While Higgins was making travel arrangements, South Vietnamese President Diem was rapidly losing what little public support he once had. On May 8, 1963, several thousand Buddhists met in Hue to celebrate their founder's 2,527th birthday. Buddha's followers were openly discriminated against by Diem's government, which was led primarily by Catholics. For instance, Buddhists had been denied the right to display their religious flags or to read statements that hadn't been approved by officials. Shortly after the celebrants gathered in Hue, they were told to go home. When they refused to do so, Diem's soldiers began to fire into the crowd. In the panic that followed, one woman and eight children were killed.

Buddhists then led demonstrations to protest Diem's cruelty. These protests also were broken up by government troops.

Refusing to surrender, some monks planned a deadly demonstration for June 11. On that day a monk sat down at a busy intersection in Saigon and prayed while one colleague dowsed him with gasoline and another set him on fire. A photographer had been alerted to this demonstration hours before, and the picture that he took of the monk's death appeared in major newspapers all over the world. Needless to say, readers were shocked.

When more monks and a nun set themselves on fire later that month, Diem's men raided more than two thousand pagodas and

Marguerite Higgins interviews Brigadier General John Beadley in Korea in 1951, the year she won the Pulitzer Prize for foreign correspondence.

temples to arrest Buddhist leaders. Diem desperately wanted to end the fiery deaths that were bringing international condemnation upon his regime. He denied that he had done anything wrong, and he blamed the Viet Cong for the deaths, insisting that they had influenced—and used—the monks.

Marguerite Higgins found the situation in Vietnam confusing at best when she arrived in July 1963. After she had talked to monks, peasants, and military advisors, she wrote a number of articles for *The New York Herald Tribune*, and later for *Newsday*, in which she tried to make sense of what she saw and to alert Americans to the turmoil she was witnessing. She told readers that the Buddhist monks were not demonstrating for religious freedom as they had said. Instead, they were part of a well-organized political plot to put Diem in the worst possible light. She noted that the so-called spontaneous demonstrations were announced well in advance so that correspondents always knew where to go and when to arrive. The monks even had handouts for the reporters. Since when, Higgins wanted to know, had political activism and violence become part of the Buddhist faith?

Higgins also chided reporters who, after the battle at Ap Bac, were beginning to predict that the South Vietnamese couldn't win. One battle didn't prove anything, she argued. She had been assured time and again by numerous advisors that the Vietnamese were capable of defeating their enemies.

Shortly after, Diem cracked down on the Buddhists, arresting more monks. American advisors, appalled and deeply embarrassed by Diem's latest actions, tried to persuade him to change his ways. When he refused to do so, U.S. officials secretly plotted with South Vietnamese army officials to remove Diem and his advisors. The coup d'état took place on November 2, 1963. Diem was not only forced out of office, he was murdered.

Marguerite Higgins was saddened by Diem's death. She genuinely believed that he had been misjudged, for when she had talked to peasants in the fields, they had told her about numerous reforms

Diem had started that had been helpful. She also thought that he had been made a scapegoat, someone to blame for the fact that the Viet Cong hadn't been defeated. Her views shocked some correspondents. How, they wondered, could she possibly draw such conclusions?

What both Higgins and her detractors sometimes failed to realize was that the situation in Vietnam was very complex, and situations varied from place to place and even from day to day. Reporters who watched events in Saigon saw a different war than did correspondents like Higgins who visited villages far away. And reporters who witnessed victories saw hope, not despair.

Different interpretations of events were not limited to journalists, however. When President Kennedy sent two advisors to study the war, one man returned with the firm belief that all was going well; the other thought that the war was a disaster. Kennedy wondered if the men had gone to the same country.

The end result of these conflicting reports was confusion; Americans on the home front didn't know what to think. Even editors who received daily reports found it difficult to find the truth. Government officials in Washington, D.C., presented information during routine press briefings that conflicted with what reporters in Vietnam were saying. This caused constant conflict between war correspondents and their editors, who often accepted the officials' version of the war. In fact, more than one reporter threatened to quit when his or her article didn't appear in the paper.

On Higgins's tenth trip to Vietnam in November 1965 (she had been in Vietnam six times before the war began) and eight months after the first American troops had arrived, she became ill. After many tests, her doctors concluded that she had leishmaniasis, a tropical disease that infects one's liver and spleen. Marguerite Higgins died on January 3, 1966.

Martha Gellhorn, another seasoned war correspondent, went to Vietnam shortly after Higgins's death. Gellhorn had covered battles in Spain, Finland, and China, and the massive bombing of London by the Nazis in World War II. Therefore she could compare the conflict in Vietnam to other wars, and she readily did so. What she saw in Vietnam, she told anyone who would listen, appalled her. Gellhorn went into the country, where she was stunned by the depth of suffering of the South Vietnamese people. In past wars, soldiers had fought soldiers, and as much as possible, civilians had been spared. But in this conflict, civilians seemed to be bearing the brunt of the war. Every family she met had suffered a fatality.

When Gellhorn spoke to relief workers, she was told again and again that the nationwide search-and-destroy efforts now conducted by American and South Vietnamese forces—especially the repeated bombings to drive out the Viet Cong or to destroy their supply routes—had not only failed but had killed and wounded thousands of unarmed men, women, and children. The bombings also terrorized some civilians to the point of actually driving them mad and so angered others that they had joined the Viet Cong.

Gellhorn was determined to tell her readers about the sights and horrors she had seen. However, her editors at the *St. Louis Post-Dispatch* and *The Ladies' Home Journal* were hesitant to print some of her most graphic reports, especially those describing disfigured children. Her editors may have been afraid of upsetting readers or appearing disloyal to the war effort. Whatever their reason for refusing her work, it didn't stop Gellhorn. She sent the reports to the *Guardian*, a newspaper in London. This paper ran nine of her most controversial articles, including "A New Kind of War," "Orphans of All Ages," and "The Uprooted."

When Gellhorn wondered aloud why some anti-Communists, especially government officials, were suddenly becoming rich or why so little of the aid Americans were sending to the Vietnamese people was reaching them, South Vietnamese officials bristled. When she announced that what she had seen had appalled her to such a degree that she could understand why the Viet Cong were gaining more and more supporters and that if she were younger she would join them, too, South Vietnamese officials were outraged. As a result, when Gellhorn returned to the United States shortly afterward to meet with her editors, South Vietnamese officials took advantage of the

Dickey Chapelle,
Photographer

Dickey Chapelle, whose real name was Georgette Louise Meyer, was an experienced war photographer. During World War II she covered the U.S. Marines' invasion of Iwo Jima and Okinawa. She also covered an uprising against the Communists in Hungary in 1956, and the revolution in Cuba that began the same year. Chapelle was not shy. She promoted herself to editors as a woman who would get the whole story. She had, she told editors, "stayed the longest and gone further forward than any reporter, man or woman."[1] Her work appeared regularly in *Life*, *Reader's Digest*, and *National Geographic*.

Chapelle began covering events in Vietnam in 1961. She did not ask for favors. When she was in the field with the soldiers, she ate the same food they did and slogged through the mud without complaint, no easy task for a woman in her late forties trying to keep up with men, who, on average, were nineteen years old. On November 4, 1965, while she was on patrol with the marines, a land mine exploded. Shrapnel from the mine hit Chapelle, severing an artery. She died shortly after.

Dickey Chapelle poses with her camera and an automatic rifle

situation. They blacklisted her, and she was denied reentry into the country for the rest of the war.

Because Higgins and Gellhorn were experienced war correspondents, they had little trouble getting their editors to send them to Saigon. However, less experienced female reporters still had to convince their editors that they could cover events in war-torn Vietnam.

One of the women who successfully convinced her supervisor to send her to Saigon was Tracy Wood. She worked for United Press International, a news service. When Wood arrived in Vietnam, her bureau chief said that he would never let her cover combat. Wood then enlisted the help of Barney Seibert in the bureau, who agreed to help her file her copy so that the chief wouldn't know who was writing the story. Wood knew that her supervisor would eventually find out that she was in the field, but she hoped that her accomplishments would convince him to let her continue. Her gamble paid off.

Her chief's acceptance didn't necessarily mean that military personnel would welcome her, though. When she was sent to a base south of Da Nang that was under great pressure from the Viet Cong, the American commander was irate when he saw Wood. "He took it as a personal offense that anyone would send a woman to cover that story. He didn't care who I was with. The idea that I was a woman sent him into a rage."[2] A more sympathetic major took her aside and helped her get her story.

In some cases, women who were denied permission quit their jobs and went to Vietnam as freelancers, selling their work to any publication that would take it. Anne Allen, whose husband was also a journalist, was a freelancer. She concentrated on stories about civilians in Saigon. Jurate Kazickas, who left her position at *Look* magazine, accompanied soldiers on their patrols into the jungle. On March 8, 1968, Kazickas was wounded. As soon as she was able, she went back to work.

Vietnam was the first war to be covered on television. Cameramen and reporters on the scene risked their lives to get footage and information to help the American public better understand what was happening. What Americans on the home front saw was the uncensored reality of war. The horror of battle appeared in people's living rooms every night on the evening news, and the sights shocked them.

Because actual filming and reporting for the cameras involved being close to combat, most of the handful of female television reporters who went to Vietnam were sent there with even greater reluctance on the part of their supervisors than was faced by reporters from the print media, and only after some lengthy arguments. The first female television journalist to go to Vietnam was Liz Trotta, a correspondent for NBC.

Liz Trotta pleaded with supervisors for months, putting copies of Higgins's Pulitzer Prize-winning articles on their desks to back her case. Her major obstacle was Ron Steinman, the bureau chief in Saigon. According to Trotta's boss, "Steinman says he'll be on the first plane back if we send a woman in there."[3] Trotta did not go to Vietnam until August 1968, more than a year after she had made her request and after Steinman had moved to another bureau.

Trotta covered numerous battles. Her first was a battle at Tay Ninh. She and her cameraman, Vo Huynh, were in position when a North Vietnamese battalion moved in. "Most of the 3,000 villagers," Liz recalled, "had fled during the night. A few terrified stragglers ran as American air strikes 'softened up' the area with 750-pound (340-kilogram) bombs and napalm. . . . The planes were working very close in, close enough for anyone on the ground to be hit by 'friendly fire' if the coordinates were off by a single degree."[4]

Trotta found the situation so frightening that she refused to stand up in front of the camera to give her report when Vo Huynh suggested that she do so. There was, he told her, lots of action, good pictures, and good light. Finally realizing that she had to take chances, she agreed to do a crouching standup, a pose that became quite common during combat when bullets were whizzing overhead.

Print journalists didn't have to worry about their appearance, but television journalists did. Even under fire, Trotta was concerned about her image. "As I spoke into the camera," she said, "I thought of the mud on my face, the greasy traces of old lipstick, and the sweat pouring down my face into the open collar of my filthy shirt. [My supervisor] would undoubtedly send me a memo about my hair."[5] Eventually Liz Trotta adjusted to the war zone so well that she volunteered for a second tour.

How many of the hundreds of correspondents—about six hundred at the height of the war—were women is not known, in large part because of the number of women working as freelance reporters who did not have an organization keeping track of them. All, especially those in the field, risked their lives. Some were wounded; two, Kate Webb and Elizabeth Pond, were taken prisoner; and at least one, Dickey Chapelle, was killed.

Their work was generally well received. Some of the women won awards for their reports, including *New York Times* correspondent Gloria Emerson, who won the George Polk Award for excellence in foreign reporting in 1971. Tad Bartimus, who worked for the Associated Press in Vietnam in 1973 and 1974, was made that organization's state bureau chief in Alaska after the war. She was the first woman to be assigned to such a position. But by far, the greatest recognition came from the home front. Like the reports of their male colleagues, the women's information mobilized the public. After watching or reading the news, Americans chose sides and drew battlelines. There was, as reporters learned when they returned to the United States, a different sort of war on the home front.

It's the warmongers against

the peaceniks.

WINNIE SMITH, U.S. ARMY

ON THE HOME FRONT 6

In past wars, government officials had rallied the American public. Presidents explained why the United States was declaring war, and then, knowing that America could not win an all-out conflict without support on the home front, they appealed to the public to back its men in uniform. Patriotic Americans rolled up their sleeves. They worked overtime to make weapons, assemble planes, and sell bonds to raise money. In fact, the drives to support war efforts became so popular that if there were people who opposed the efforts, few were willing to risk the wrath of their neighbors to say so.

But when the United States became involved in the war in Vietnam, government officials did not wage a campaign to win the hearts and minds of Americans. Although there were some pacifists in the United States who opposed all wars and some critics who thought that the conflict in Vietnam was a civil war best settled by the Vietnamese themselves, officials knew that the vast majority of the public—some polls said 80 percent of Americans—believed that sending troops to Vietnam was the right thing to do. Furthermore, since the war was likely to be short because the Viet Cong and the North Vietnamese were not great military powers, there appeared to be little need to enlist support on the home front.

Even though few Americans questioned the reason behind U.S. intervention in Vietnam at the beginning of the war, many became upset by how the war was being fought. Officials had assured the public that airmen were targeting only military installations or Communist supply lines, but pictures of burning villages and fleeing refugees proved otherwise. Journalists' stories about the use of napalm also worried the public. Worse yet, rumors began to surface about over-eager search-and-destroy missions in the South that resulted in the deaths of innocent civilians. In one instance in 1968, every man, woman, and child—more than three hundred people— were slaughtered in My Lai by U.S. troops. War had never been pretty, but this conflict struck many Americans as especially nasty.

In addition, the contradictory accounts of battles—who won and who really lost—began to worry the public. When the Communists launched their stunning and successful Tet offensive in 1968, Americans began to wonder if the war could be won. If not, they asked, why send more men to fight?

Americans became even more concerned in 1969 when they finally learned, thanks to the efforts of the media, that the United States had engaged in secret operations in nearby Cambodia. These operations had included bombing even more villages. Now polls indicated that 60 percent of the American public thought that sending troops to Asia was a mistake.

In 1971, concern turned to outrage. Two newspapers, *The New York Times* and *The Washington Post*, published what became known as the Pentagon Papers. This lengthy report, seven thousand pages long, was given to the newspapers by Daniel Ellsberg, an employee in the Defense Department. These papers were copies of government documents that showed that the reports about the attack on the

U.S.S. *Maddox* had been deliberately exaggerated so that the United States had an excuse to send soldiers to Vietnam. The papers also proved that the United States had been involved in the downfall of Diem's government and that the numerous bombings of North Vietnam had done little to weaken the North's army, contrary to what U.S. officials had said. In short, officials, including several presidents, had repeatedly lied to the American people. Polls taken in 1971 indicated that now 70 percent of Americans wanted the United States to immediately withdraw its troops.

The first antiwar resistance in America took place only weeks after the United States sent its first soldiers to Vietnam, and it began on college campuses. Student dissent, to the dismay of many parents, had been growing for several years. Some rebellious students had questioned Americans' values, especially the quest for the biggest house on the block. Instead, these students believed that their calling was to find ways to make life better for all. So they threw themselves into the civil-rights struggle and the war against poverty. Their mottoes were "justice," "love," and above all, "peace."

Some young adults also challenged authority and demanded a greater voice in what they were learning in school, much of which they considered irrelevant to their new lifestyles. When administrators failed to take the students seriously, they organized protests. In addition, they started organizations, such as Students for a Democratic Society, to help them achieve their goals. These organizations, composed of men and women, most of whom never made it into history books, served as the nucleus for the student antiwar movement.

Because so many conflicting reports were being given, students attended teach-ins to try to learn as much as possible about the war. The first teach-in, held on March 24, 1965, was organized by faculty members at the University of Michigan at Ann Arbor. Instructors and students alike, especially young men who were eligible for the draft, had become deeply concerned about the war when President Johnson announced that he was sending American troops to Asia.

This Vietnam War protest took place in New York City on New Year's Day 1967 and included nearly 100,000 demonstrators.

The Poverty of our Foreign Policy is Causing War

END THE DRAFT—
LET YOUNG MEN LIVE

STOP THE WAR NOW!

INSUFFICIENT

I AM NOT A COMMUNIST AND I STILL OPPOSE THE WAR IN VIETNAM

OUR BOYS ARE DYING

THE PEOPLE OF THE UNITED STATES WOULD OK OVER THEIR TIONALISTIC, REAC-ONARY PRIDE, THE AR WOULD BE OVER.

CAN BE WRONG

BIG
GE
GIS

Teachers at Ann Arbor hoped that at least a few hundred students would attend the lectures; instead, more than three thousand came to hear the speakers, many of whom questioned America's right to try to keep an unpopular government in power. This was, these speakers argued, an attempt to force what was best for America upon other people. Furthermore, given the history of Vietnam, the fighting would continue indefinitely, destroying the country and killing millions of people in the process, including many Americans. What, the speakers wondered, was to be gained by that?

The teach-in at Ann Arbor was so well received that instructors and students at other colleges quickly followed suit. The largest teach-in, organized by two graduate students at the University of California at Berkeley, Jerry Rubin and Barbara Gullahorn, attracted at least 20,000 participants who listened to a thirty-six-hour debate about the growing crisis in Asia. On May 15, 1965, a national teach-in took place in Washington, D.C. During the debates, many students became convinced that American soldiers should be withdrawn from Vietnam as soon as possible.

Understandably, the teach-ins alarmed government officials. Afraid that their side was being presented unfairly or not at all, they sent "truth-teams" to universities to talk to students. But it was too late. Government reports were already being questioned, and students simply refused to believe much—if anything—that team members said.

Teach-ins were just the beginning. Students held a dizzying array of marches and rallies and started organizations whose sole purpose was to end the war in Vietnam. First and foremost, students, through peaceful demonstrations, tried to persuade government officials to withdraw troops from Asia. When withdrawal failed to materialize, thousands of young men and women worked for antiwar political candidates, such as Eugene McCarthy, who promised to end the war. When these candidates failed to win, students tried to reduce the number of soldiers available by encouraging young men not to register for the draft, which was renewed in 1967, or to refuse to go when called.

Antiwar students also tried to hamper the war effort by attempting to sever all connections between their campuses and the armed services, as well as cutting all ties between their schools and any businesses that supplied war matériel. Students began this massive effort by trying to end Reserve Officers Training Corps (ROTC) programs, which prepared young men for the army reserve while they were attending college, on campuses. Protesters also tried to persuade university administrators to eliminate programs that conducted research for the military. And finally, antiwar students tried to prevent representatives from companies that made weapons, napalm, and another defoliant, Agent Orange, from holding job interviews on school grounds. Success varied greatly from campus to campus.

Being part of the antiwar movement was never easy, but it was especially difficult in the beginning when most Americans, following tradition, supported the war. More than a few adults thought that antiwar students were spoiled brats looking for trouble (President Nixon called them "bums") or, worse yet, Communists who were trying to undermine America's resolve to win the war. Women who participated in antiwar demonstrations were thought to be without morals, and the men who marched were regarded as traitors who wouldn't fight for their country when asked to do so.

Therefore the first demonstrations were not well received. Bystanders attacked the marchers with raw eggs and rotten fruit, tore demonstrators' signs from their hands, and when that failed to stop them, beat them with their fists. When the police moved in to keep order, the demonstrators were arrested for disturbing the peace.

The protesters didn't quit, though. By 1967, antiwar groups existed on many college campuses, and representatives from these groups were working together to stage massive rallies. In October, for example, at least 50,000 demonstrators met in Washington, D.C., to march on the Pentagon, headquarters of the Defense Department.

But no matter how impressive the demonstrations were, the students, and the growing number of adults who joined them, were unable to persuade the government to withdraw from Asia. As a result, many frustrated students turned from protest to civil disobedience to further their cause. They copied some of the most successful techniques used by civil-rights workers. This usually involved marching without permits or in larger numbers than allowed and blocking the doors of induction centers where would-be soldiers reported for enlistment. The new demonstrations interfered with officials and gained lots of publicity, but they did not end the war.

By 1968, a handful of students, convinced that the government would never respond to the peoples' wishes, thought that violence was the answer. Some of these students caused confrontations during demonstrations, especially at the National Democratic Convention in August. Others believed that a revolution was needed. These extremists destroyed property and killed a young researcher at the University of Wisconsin when they blew up a science building. Their violent acts cast suspicion on all students who opposed the war and gave some Americans an excuse to ignore their message, at least for a while.

On April 30, 1970, President Nixon announced that South Vietnamese troops with the help of American airmen, had actually invaded Cambodia, expanding the ground war. The invasion enraged students. After five years of protesting, students not only had failed to bring an end to the war, but they had been unable to prevent it from escalating.

Massive protests erupted at many universities, but best remembered is the one at Kent State University in Ohio. Antiwar organizers planned to hold a rally at noon on Friday, May 1, to protest the invasion of Cambodia. They knew that they couldn't force a withdrawal, but they at least wanted to try one more time to shut down the ROTC center on campus. By the end of the rally, emotions were running high.

That Saturday evening someone set the ROTC building on fire. When fire trucks arrived, students cut the hoses and then skirmished with police who tried to restore order. The governor of Ohio, James Rhodes, announced a state of emergency, banned demonstrations, and brought in the National Guard, which was heavily armed. More

This 1971 poster publicizes a demonstration sponsored by the United Women's Contingent. Protests were to be held in both San Francisco and Washington, D.C.

angry than ever, students planned a rally for noon on Monday, May 4, to protest the expansion of the war, the presence of the National Guard, and the restrictions placed on demonstrations.

Tension mounted throughout the morning of May 4 as students gathered near the commons. Shortly after noon, guardsmen told students to disperse. Unarmed students responded by throwing rocks at the men and telling them to go home. Determined to break up the crowd, soldiers fired tear gas at the students. When the students ran, a small group of guardsmen followed some of them a short distance before deciding to retreat. Students threw more rocks at these men, who suddenly stopped, turned, and pointed their rifles at the students. The men then turned again, walked a few steps up a nearby hill, suddenly swung around, and fired in unison. When the shooting was over, nine students were wounded, and four—Allison Beth Krause, Jeffrey Glenn Miller, Sandra Lee Scheuer, and William K. Schroeder—were dead.

Reaction across the country was swift and divided. Most students were horrified. Some Americans who thought that protesters were traitors believed that the dead students had gotten exactly what they deserved.

But the investigations that followed put the blame on the guardsmen. The Justice Department's inquiry concluded that the men were never in real danger. Therefore shooting to kill was not necessary, especially since the soldiers could have resorted to using more tear gas to protect themselves. One member of another investigation, the Scranton Commission, believed that at least two guardsmen had gone to Kent State with the intent of shooting at the students and that the men had used the rock-tossing incidents as an excuse to fire.[1]

Although many Americans thought that demonstrations would stop after the deaths at Kent State, that was not the case. Irate students protested all over the country, shutting down more than four hundred campuses. Later that month, when a major demonstration for all antiwar groups was slated for Washington, D.C., students showed up in large numbers—only now they were beginning to take precautions.

Norma Becker, a demonstration coordinator, was amazed at the turnout in Washington, especially since students had good reason to believe that they might be assaulted. She recalled that students wore helmets and "came prepared for heavy-duty action. . . . They were out there to express . . . outrage at a government policy that was slaughtering people in Vietnam and was now killing students on American campuses. . . . They were prepared to be arrested, they were prepared to be hurt."[2]

While many ridiculed the antiwar movement led by young adults, at least in the beginning, few could make light of the organization known as Women Strike for Peace (WSP). The WSPs (pronounced "wisps"), middle-aged women, most of whom were mothers, made a dignified appearance in their tailored suits, strings of pearls, and high-heeled shoes. In addition, these women, 50,000 strong, had political know-how and clout. Besides being leaders in their communities, they had helped persuade American officials to sign treaties with Communist leaders that would limit the development and testing of nuclear weapons, which was a popular cause in the United States.

WSP became involved in the antiwar movement in the mid-1960s, shortly after college students began to make their beliefs known. Because so many Americans looked down upon the students, WSP decided not to unite with the student movement. Instead, members held informal meetings in their homes, inviting neighbors over for coffee and a discussion about the war. The women also handed out leaflets in shopping centers and on street corners and sent representatives to Washington to talk to officials.

WSP members believed that the best way to stop the war was to persuade young men to defy the draft. So members set up counseling centers, met buses coming to induction centers so that they could talk to men planning to enlist, and used their influence in their communities, where many were active in PTAs, to talk to high-school students about the war.

Men who refused to be inducted into the armed services and who did not subsequently flee the country were jailed unless they could prove that fighting violated their religious beliefs. WSP supported

WSP members carry posters decrying the violence in
Vietnam during their protest at the Pentagon in
Washington, D.C., on February 16, 1967.

the men who resisted the draft by appearing at their court hearings,
visiting them in jail, and organizing letter-writing campaigns to make
sure that the men were not forgotten.

But no matter how many men the WSP kept from enlisting—they
claimed that thousands had been persuaded to resist—the war went on.
So in 1967, the women, like the antiwar students, decided to take
bolder actions to get the government to withdraw troops from Vietnam.

On February 16, more than two thousand WSP members, some
with young children in tow, marched to the Defense Department,
where WSP leaders had been told they would be able to talk to

department officials. But when the women arrived, they found all the doors bolted. This wasn't the first time that they had been denied an audience with leaders. The women were so angry that some of them took off their high heels and began to beat on the doors. Others shouted to the officials to come out. In the process, the women created quite a stir, and photographers began to snap pictures while reporters described the scene. When the angry women finally withdrew, reporters wondered about the presence of children in a demonstration. WSP leader Dagmar Wilson, unrepentant, replied, "Some people take their children to churches. We take ours to marches."[3]

Refusing to be ignored, WSP held another demonstration that year. On September 20, one thousand members began their protest by carrying a coffin draped with a banner stating "Not My Son, Not Your Son, Not Their Sons" to the headquarters of the Selective Service, the organization in charge of the draft. They encountered no resistance.

After depositing the coffin, they proceeded to the White House to find a line of policemen blocking their access to the gate. Believing that they had the right to demonstrate on property owned by the people and defying a new rule that said only one hundred could picket at one time, the women decided to make a dash for the gate, pushing their way past the policemen, who were taken by surprise. When a second line of policemen suddenly appeared, waving clubs in the air, the women sat down in the road. They would have continued to block traffic until they were arrested, but two WSP leaders, Bella Abzug and Dagmar Wilson, persuaded them that little could be gained by their arrests. It would be better, the leaders said, to resume picketing. The women eventually—and half-heartedly—agreed to do so.

Many WSP members also belonged to another antiwar group, the Women's International League for Peace and Freedom (WILPF). This group made a strong effort to reach out to African-American women involved in the civil-rights movement. In doing so, WILPF gained the support of several famous leaders, including Coretta Scott King.

Mary Beth Tinker

Mary Beth and John Tinker display the black armbands that brought the sister and brother before the U.S. Supreme Court in 1968.

Mary Beth Tinker stood firm against America's involvement in the war. On December 16, 1965, thirteen-year-old Mary Beth, her fifteen-year-old brother, John, and a friend, Chris Eckhardt, wore black armbands to their schools in Des Moines, Iowa, to show their opposition to American troops being in Vietnam. Their principals were afraid that the sight of the bands might cause a disturbance in the classrooms, and the students were told to remove them. When the Tinkers and Eckhardt refused to do so, they were suspended.

These teenagers believed that their First Amendment rights had been violated, and they sought help from the Iowa Civil Liberties Union. The union agreed to help them, taking their case all the way to the U.S. Supreme Court. In 1969, the Court, by a vote of seven to two, decided in favor of the students. Peaceful dissent, even in school, was determined to be permissible.

Coretta Scott King speaks at a peace rally in New York City a few weeks after her husband, Martin Luther King Jr., was murdered in 1968. She recited "ten commandments" on Vietnam that were found among the slain leader's papers.

Coretta Scott King, wife of civil-rights leader Martin Luther King Jr., had long been an advocate for peace. She had been a WSP delegate to an international convention in Switzerland in 1962 that promoted limiting nuclear weapons, and in 1963 she had demonstrated against nuclear weapons in front of the United Nations. By 1965, she was a featured speaker at numerous antiwar demonstrations.

Although King objected to all wars, she found this one especially troubling, calling the war in Vietnam "the most . . . evil war in the history of mankind."[4]

King was deeply disturbed by the death and destruction that the war was causing. She also believed that poor black American soldiers, many of whom had been drafted, were shouldering the burden in Vietnam. She repeatedly pointed out that young men from wealthier families could afford to go to college, where they would be exempt from service for four years. In addition, King listed a number of social ills in the United States, including extreme poverty among blacks. She wondered aloud if the money being poured into Asia couldn't be put to better use in America.

Fannie Lou Hamer, another African-American woman, also opposed the war. She scoffed when told that American soldiers were fighting for democracy in Vietnam, pointing out the oppressive actions of the South Vietnamese leaders. Hamer was fighting for voting rights for blacks in Mississippi, a dangerous thing to do at that time. At the height of the struggle in the mid-1960s, during which civil-rights activists were repeatedly threatened, Hamer told President Johnson that he should withdraw U.S. troops in Vietnam and reassign them to the South to protect the people who were really fighting for democracy.

Antiwar protesters kept putting the issue of the war before the public, and by the late 1960s gained support from many Americans. By that time, the fear of Communist expansion had lessened, in part because of the Communists' willingness to discuss limits on nuclear weapons. Also, the news from Vietnam was anything but good, and few Americans honestly believed that there was anything to be gained by continuing to fight. Students and women were eventually joined by union members (some of whom had opposed student protesters only a few years before), church leaders, businessmen, some veterans returning from the war, and volunteers from relief organizations. Leaders of the International Voluntary Services, for example, resigned from their positions in Vietnam to show their opposition to the war.

Norma Becker

Norma Becker believed in equality and peace. Before joining the antiwar movement, she fought for equal rights for blacks. When American troops were sent to Vietnam, Becker immediately began to organize demonstrations in New York to try to persuade the government to rethink its policy in Asia. Becker, a teacher in New York City, took charge of New York's Fifth Avenue Parade Committee, one of the largest antiwar groups in the area. In addition to coordinating demonstrations, Becker also organized civil disobedience events, including blocking entrances to local induction centers.

Even famous movie stars like Jane Fonda joined the antiwar movement. Fonda traveled throughout the United States, giving slide shows to Americans about the effects of the war on the Vietnamese. She also supported the protesters who were putting pressure on Congress to cut off funding for the war. In 1972, Fonda went to North Vietnam, where she praised the efforts of the Communists to reunite the two sections and announced that American soldiers should not be fighting in Vietnam. Her comments raised the ire of all supporters of the war and made her one of the most controversial protesters in America.

But even though the antiwar movement grew more and more powerful in the late 1960s and early 1970s, no president wanted to be the first in American history to lose a war, so the fighting continued. As long as there were troops in the field, there was hope of either pulling off a decisive victory or at least gaining enough ground to be able to negotiate a favorable peace treaty. Besides, incredible as it may seem, leaders, especially President Nixon, still believed that the majority of Americans supported the war effort no matter what the polls said. Nixon argued that these people did not shout their support, instead they went about their business as usual. He called them "the silent majority." One woman and her two daughters disagreed with Nixon's assessment of the situation. During a demonstration they carried a banner that read, "The majority isn't silent. The government is deaf."[5]

When the number of people at antiwar rallies swelled to more than 750,000, even President Nixon had to admit that the war was not popular. He and his advisors then developed a new policy, "Vietnamization." Vietnamization meant that American troops would be withdrawn over time, and well-armed South Vietnamese soldiers would take their place.

Although more and more Americans joined the antiwar movement over the years, not all did so. Diehard supporters of the war considered the movement unpatriotic and dangerous. Supporters believed that the marches and rallies convinced the Communists that the United States was deeply divided and therefore weak, encouraging the Communists to continue to fight. Furthermore, supporters believed that protesters undermined the morale of the soldiers in Asia, making them less effective than they might have been. In addition, supporters argued that protesters tied the hands of government officials who should have waged an all-out war but were afraid to do so because of the uproar such actions would have caused. Therefore, when the war ended in defeat, more than one supporter blamed antiwar Americans.

Supporters of the war also held rallies and organized demonstrations. In 1967, supporters asked all patriots to join them in Loyalty Day parades in New York. Although organizers hoped to have more than 100,000 participants, only 7,500 showed up. The parade went ahead anyway, with many American flags to counter the North Vietnamese flags that some protesters carried, and banners that read, "One Country, one flag. Love it or leave it."[6] By late 1968, after the Communists' successful Tet offensive that shook American confidence, and revelations about the My Lai massacre, the number of supporters dwindled dramatically.

Not all demonstrations were against the war, and women were among those who rallied in favor of the effort. These students gathered in New York City in October 1967.

Perhaps no group was more concerned about the protesters than the families of American prisoners of war (POWs). The first prisoners—most of them pilots who had bombed North Vietnam—were captured in 1965, and their numbers grew during the following years to more than a thousand. When protesters argued that the United States had no right to be in Vietnam, this played into the hands of the North Vietnamese who insisted that the captives were war criminals. As a result, the North Vietnamese not only threatened to put the captives on trial, they denied the men basic rights that warring nations in the past had agreed to provide. This included giving the captives' names to American authorities. Therefore, family members of men missing in action (MIAs) did not know if their loved ones were dead or being held in a cell in Hanoi.

American officials asked family members not to publicize the POW issue, since some of these pilots had been shot down during secret operations. But family members, rightfully fearing for the safety of their loved ones, decided to take action anyway. Wives of men thought to be prisoners formed the League of Wives of American Vietnam Prisoners of War in 1967, which eventually became the National League of Families of American POWs and MIAs. Shortly after, members started a very public campaign to help the POWs, a campaign that the Communists could not ignore.

Sybil Stockdale, whose husband was shot down in 1965, became one of the leaders of the league. She helped publicize the plight of the prisoners and eventually, with the help of a massive letter-writing campaign, brought about the exchange of mail between some of the captives and their families. The North Vietnamese, however, still refused to provide a list of all captives, insisting that it wouldn't do so until the United States withdrew from the war.

Stockdale would not accept the North's refusal, and she flew to Europe to meet with Communist officials in the fall of 1969 at the North Vietnamese embassy in Paris. She reported everything to the press, which had now taken an interest in the captives' case. The refusal of the North Vietnamese to even release names was viewed by many leaders all over the world as mean-spirited, and many publicly protested this decision. The publicity that Stockdale generated, as well as the attention given to other wives who went to Paris a few months later, put so much pressure on the North Vietnamese that they finally agreed to provide a list of the prisoners.

Anne Purcell, whose husband had been reported missing in action in early 1968 and a prisoner of war in 1969, was also a member of the league. Purcell helped publicize the prisoners' plight by handing out leaflets, asking people to sign petitions, and giving

While Gold Star Mothers banded together to mourn the loss of their children in Vietnam, women such as June Duke Gaylor, pictured here in 1995, whose son Charles Duke was declared missing in action in 1970, remains ever hopeful that her son is still alive.

Gold Star Mothers

When a soldier dies, many on the home front mourn his or her death. In 1928, Grace Darling Seibold started an organization called American Gold Star Mothers to honor one group of mourners, the mothers of sons and daughters who are killed in combat. To draw attention to these women and their loss, Siebold's organization made an old tradition in some parts of the country into a national custom. In the past when America had been at war, some parents who had children in the armed services displayed a special flag for each soldier in their homes. Usually the small white flag, bordered in red, white, and blue, had a blue star in the center. If the soldier was killed, a gold star was placed over the blue emblem to indicate the family's loss. During World War II (1941–1945), American Gold Star Mothers attempted to give each mother who had lost a child in combat a gold star. This practice continued throughout the next wars, including the war in Vietnam, during which 58,000 Americans died.

Mothers who had children in Vietnam, as had many mothers before them, worried about their sons and daughters in the armed services every day. Mrs. Marion Baker, whose son Paul Joseph Baker died in Vietnam on March 29, 1969, said:

> I think from the time Paul went to Vietnam to the day he died, every time I heard a car stop in front of the house, I went to the window thinking that [someone had come to tell me that Paul had died], so the clock was running for me, too, but the day they did come, I wasn't there. I was teaching at the high school, so they got his father first, then came to the high school to get me. . . . My husband didn't even have to tell me what had happened. They called me down to the guidance room and said, "There's someone who wants to see you." When I walked in and looked at his face, he didn't have to say anything. I knew. It's just something you're dreading happening all those months, and then it's happened, and you're numb. . . . [Paul] did what he felt he wanted to do and should do [enlist], and I think it was up to us to respect his choice.
>
> The years that he had were wonderful years, maybe not the one in Vietnam, but, while he had a short life, he achieved a lot. . . . so I don't feel bitter.[7]

Today, in addition to displaying a white flag with a gold star, Gold Star Mothers such as Mrs. Baker wear a pin, a gold star on a purple background, bordered by a gold wreath. It is hoped that all who see these pins will recognize and acknowledge the loss that these women have suffered.

The Home Front in Vietnam

By the end of 1967, the war had destroyed much of the Vietnamese countryside. In a letter to President Johnson, volunteers from the International Voluntary Services organization described the scene:

> We have flown at a safe height over the deserted villages, the sterile valleys, the forests with the huge swaths cut out, and the long-abandoned rice checks. We have had intimate contact with the refugees. Some of them get jobs at American military establishments and do fairly well. Others are forcibly resettled, landless, in isolated, desolate places which are turned into colonies of beggars. . . . In a refugee village one of us heard an old woman say . . . "These days of sorrow are filled with napalm, hate, and death. The rice fields turn brown. The new year brings a cold, clutching fear."[8]

speeches. Like so many of the group's members, she helped raise funds for the league's activities by selling bumper stickers that said "POWs Never Have a Nice Day," and "Don't Let Them Be Forgotten." She also sold POW bracelets that became so popular, even some antiwar demonstrators wore them. Each bracelet carried the name of a captive or a man missing in action. The purchaser of the bracelet promised to wear it, and thus show support for the soldier, until the Red Cross was allowed to see the prisoners in Hanoi and inform their families about their well-being. This finally occurred in 1971.

In 1973 a peace treaty was signed by the United States and North Vietnam. After the United States had withdrawn the last of its troops from Vietnam, North Vietnam released its captives, some of whom had been held for eight years. The emotional reunions touched the hearts of all Americans, protesters and supporters alike. The long, painful struggle was thought to be over.

It was a war we shouldn't have been in
. . . but the fact was we were there, and
we did the best we could.

PINKIE HOUSER, U.S. ARMY

AFTERWORD

The United States signed a treaty with the North Vietnamese on January 31, 1973, which officially ended American military action in the war and brought a temporary halt in the fighting. By the end of March, U.S. leaders had withdrawn almost all American troops, leaving only a limited number of soldiers in Saigon to defend specialists left behind to advise the South's leaders. According to the North Vietnamese, all remaining prisoners-of-war were released in April, although questions remain to this day about whether all of the men were set free.

The war between the North and South resumed in January 1974. In the following months, the North gained more and more territory. When Communist forces made a dramatic push toward the South's capital, the remaining Americans were evacuated on April 29, 1975. Saigon fell to the North Vietnamese on April 30, marking the end of the war. Vietnam was now one country under the control of the Communists.

Because the conflict in Vietnam differed so much from other wars—guerrilla warfare, the massive antiwar movement, and the defeat—it's not surprising that its aftermath was also very different. This was true for military personnel, war correspondents, and volunteers in Asia, as well as for Americans on the home front.

In the past, members of the armed services often returned home aboard military planes and ships with entire units to be greeted by crowds of well-wishers and treated to ticker-tape parades. They were heroes. Not only were there no parades for Vietnam veterans when they returned a few at a time at the end of their one-year tour (or even in large numbers at the end of the war), the people who were on hand when these veterans arrived had mixed feelings.

While family members and loved ones were joyous, some Americans were hostile toward the veterans. This was especially true at the end of the war. Many Americans were angry because the United States had lost the conflict. They were embarrassed by this, and rather than try to understand how complex and difficult the war was, some blamed the soldiers for not trying hard enough. Other Americans were appalled by how the war had been fought and the fact that so many civilians had died. These Americans had read stories about the massacre at My Lai. Believing that all soldiers had participated in such atrocities, some Americans had little respect for any of the veterans.

As a result, when military personnel, easily identifiable in their uniforms, entered airports or bus stations (most used public transportation for at least part of their trip home), people picked them out of the crowd. Most of the time veterans simply encountered silence. Occasionally, though, troublemakers targeted the veterans and harassed them, wondering aloud about how many women and children the veterans had killed, and on occasion, actually assaulting military personnel.

Even nurses were not immune to these attacks. One woman was followed all over an airport in California the entire time she was there. Her tormentors repeatedly asked her questions about where she had been and what she had done. "I know I should have stood up to them," she said later, "but it was such a shock to me. I was so happy to be home. It was a hard way to come back."[1] In another incident, an army nurse was assaulted. Shortly after she got off a plane in Los Angeles, she was knocked down by four people who called her a "fascist pig."

When stories about such encounters reached Vietnam, veterans expressed outrage and fear for their safety. Some even carried weapons to protect themselves once they were back in the United States, and more than one reported being more afraid in America than he or she had been in Vietnam.

At the end of previous wars, women in the military were mustered out as quickly as possible. But at the end of the war in Vietnam, the military actively sought more women. The draft had ended in 1973, and officials feared that enlistment would plummet, especially in light of the fact that the armed services weren't held in the highest esteem by most Americans at the time. Women had long sought careers and advancement opportunities in the military, and now that the government really wanted them, women bargained for and won significant gains. More assignments were made available, and women could attend military academies and even teach at these academies, an accomplishment that would have stunned women who two hundred years before had to pretend to be men in order to serve their country.

Military nurses did not fare as well after the war. They had dealt with wounds more gruesome than any encountered in previous conflicts, and they had endured the trauma of repeated shelling. Even so, these women had been expected to deal with their emotions on their own. Although many of the nurses somehow managed to numb their feelings during the war, it was only a matter of time before their pain, despair, and rage surfaced. Some nurses then experienced uncontrollable crying spells, nightmares, and angry outbursts. These are symptoms of an ailment known today as post-traumatic stress disorder (PTSD), which medical personnel soon realized was not limited to nurses; almost all who served in Vietnam, men and women alike, suffered from PTSD to some degree.

This disorder was very serious, but nurses had few places to turn to for help. The Veterans Administration insisted that it had its hands full dealing with the many problems that the men were facing. The nurses couldn't help each other, since most, trying to put the war behind them, had lost contact with other women who had served in Vietnam. Talking to anyone who hadn't been in the war zone was very difficult; the nurses believed that no one could possibly understand what they had endured. Besides, they weren't sure about what kind of reaction they might get if they sought outside help.

In 1978, Lynda Van Devanter, who had been a nurse in Vietnam, recognized the need for counseling and began to push for help for all women who served in Asia. The Veterans Administration finally agreed to contact as many women as possible (records were not complete), establish support groups, and set up counseling sessions. This was the first major step toward recovery for the women.

Volunteers who went to Vietnam to assist the soldiers, such as USO workers, left Asia when American troops were withdrawn in 1973. However, a number of female volunteers who worked for relief agencies in Vietnam remained until the Communists entered Saigon in 1975. Some, especially those associated with the American Friends (Quaker) relief effort, were among the last Americans to leave Asia.

Because the South fell so quickly when the North Vietnamese made their final push, some volunteers escaped only hours before Communist tanks rolled into their area. Julie Forsythe, who worked for the American Friends Service Committee in Da Nang, recalled the pandemonium as thousands fled the city: "I remember nothing but mass hysteria—people hanging off the wings of airplanes. . . . The roads were jammed. It was almost impossible to get anywhere. . . . I [left] on a barge. There were . . . hundreds of people trying to get on the barge. People pushing each other off. People throwing possessions over, throwing each other's possessions over."[2]

No longer able to help the Vietnamese in their own country, some of the volunteers helped the refugees. From 1975 to 1985, more than

1.4 million South Vietnamese, Cambodians, and Laotians, particularly those who had worked closely with American forces, left Southeast Asia. About half of these people settled in the United States with the help of federal agencies, relief organizations, and many volunteers, some of whom agreed to sponsor families or adopt orphans. Never before had the United States accepted so many refugees after a war, and without past experience, resettlement was difficult for both the refugees and their supporters. Often, the Asians were not accepted in their new communities, in part because they reminded Americans of the war they had lost.

Interestingly enough, for years women war correspondents had been told that they shouldn't get too close to combat. By the end of the Vietnam War, they were told that they hadn't been close enough. Many Americans were angry at the media because it hadn't uncovered events in a more timely fashion. For example, the public couldn't understand how the military had managed to bomb Cambodia for months, or had kept the slaughter at My Lai a secret for a whole year, when hundreds of correspondents were in the area. Other Americans railed at the press because it wasn't supportive enough of the war effort. In either case, the public no longer separated the men from the women; it treated both sexes equally, repeatedly lashing out at all correspondents. The press lost some of its credibility with average Americans during the war, and the media struggled for years to try to regain the status it had enjoyed at the end of previous wars, even though, ironically, it had not always told the truth in the past.

On the other hand, government officials developed a real fear of the press during the war. The media may have been slow in uncovering some of the government's actions, but it had eventually discovered and exposed secret operations. Also, when the government fought to put limits on the press and stop the publication of the Pentagon Papers, the U.S. Supreme Court had backed the press. In this way, the media had became more powerful than ever.

The role of the home front in previous wars had always been one of support, not confrontation. At the end of a war, millions of women who had worked in war industries went home, ending their involvement in the conflict. Returning soldiers filled the vacancies in these plants, many of which started to manufacture household goods again.

But because the home front had not been mobilized to the extent it had been in either World War or during the Korean conflict, there weren't millions of jobs to be had after Vietnam. In fact, the economy was in a serious slump, which would only get worse when the government stopped buying helicopters and grenades. As a result, veterans had difficulty finding work. This was one of the major reasons that female veterans considered staying in the armed services when their tour of duty ended.

Although the home front became silent after previous wars had ended, antiwar advocates had no intention of losing their voices. Few protesters trusted government officials now, and their trust was shaken even more, if that was possible, during the Watergate scandal that led to President Nixon's resignation in 1974. Antiwar leaders kept an eye on government officials to make sure that the United States really did withdraw all of its armed forces from Vietnam, then set out to cut off further funding for South Vietnam.

In addition, as other international hot spots developed in the coming years, antiwar leaders shouted: "No More Vietnams!" This did not mean that America would not participate in peacekeeping missions or refuse to help a country that had been invaded by its neighbor. It meant that military leaders had to have clearly defined goals in mind and a reasonable expectation of winning a conflict or taking control of a situation before troops could be sent.

Many women who had been involved in the antiwar movement also used their organizational and demonstration skills to further the cause of equal rights for women. Although they made significant gains in educational and employment opportunities, they failed to achieve one of their most cherished goals, the passage of the Equal Rights Amendment.

*Woman Vietnam veterans support each other following the 1993
dedication of the Women's Memorial in Washington, D.C.
Created by sculptor Glenna Goodacre, it depicts two nurses
tending a fallen soldier.*

On January 25, 1981, fifty-two American hostages who had been
held in Teheran, Iran, for more than a year were finally released. All
Americans were greatly relieved that the situation had ended peace-
fully, and when the men and women arrived in the United States,
they were welcomed as heroes. The parades, speeches, and celebrations upset Vietnam veterans because they were reminders of how
America had ignored the veterans' own sacrifices. Where, they
wanted to know, was their parade?

Veterans then decided to raise money for a memorial to honor the men and women who had served in Vietnam. By this time, Americans had had some time to reflect upon the war and learn more about the conflict. As a result, they were more aware of the sacrifices that U.S. soldiers and their supporters had made. So when Congress granted the memorial committee the right to erect a monument in Washington, D.C., there was little objection. The memorial, an impressive long black granite wall with the names of all who had died in the conflict chiseled into the stone, was dedicated on Veterans Day, November 11, 1982. The dedication service included parades, speeches, and emotional reunions among soldiers who had not seen each other since they left Vietnam. In 1984, a statue of three male soldiers was dedicated.

Diane Carlson Evans, an army nurse during the war, was among those who attended the services at the Vietnam Veterans Memorial and the dedication of the statue. Evans thought that a women's memorial should be added. Working with the nurses identified by Lynda Van Devanter's push to get counseling for female veterans, Evans started a drive to erect the Vietnam Women's Memorial. The women held fund-raisers, talked to government officials, and encountered more obstacles than they could have imagined when they began working toward their goal. But on Veterans Day, 1993, the Vietnam Women's Memorial was finally dedicated.

The Wall and the Memorial are among the most frequently visited sites in the nation's capital today. While many visitors are curious tourists and people too young to remember the war, the memorials are special places for former supporters of the war and antiwar protesters alike, providing sites where the women can reflect upon the conflict and how it changed their lives. Visiting the memorials also gives women who served on the home front or in Vietnam an opportunity to reflect upon their efforts and to realize and say aloud, as Pinkie Houser did, "We did the best we could."[3] Little more could have been asked, even from the valiant women of the Vietnam War.

TIMELINE

1954   Vietnam is divided into two parts.

1955   The United States sends aid and advisors to South Vietnam.

1956   Dwight D. Eisenhower is elected president. When the Viet Cong push for elections, South Vietnamese officials crack down on their opponents.

1959   North Vietnam sends weapons to the Viet Cong on the Ho Chi Minh trail.

1960   Newly elected President John F. Kennedy promises to help South Vietnam.

1963   Battle at Ap Bac takes place in January. First Buddhist monk is set on fire in June. Diem is overthrown in November.

1964   Lyndon B. Johnson is elected president. About 15,000 American advisors are now in Vietnam. The U.S.S. *Maddox* is attacked by North Vietnamese on August 2. U.S. retaliates with bombing raids in North Vietnam.

1965   The first WACs arrive in Vietnam in January. The first American combat troops (3,500) and first army nurses arrive in March. First teach-in is held in March in Michigan. First navy nurses arrive in Asia in October. Volunteers to help soldiers and civilians begin to arrive in Vietnam.

1966   By the end of December, American troops number 400,000.

1967   Women Strike for Peace demonstrates in February. Women Marines arrive in Vietnam in March. First Loyalty Day Parades are held. First WAF officers arrive in the fall. March on the Pentagon occurs in October. Wives of prisoners of war form League of Wives of American POWs.

1968   Communists launch Tet offensive in January. My Lai massacre takes place in March. Richard M. Nixon is elected president in November. More than 500,000 American soldiers are stationed in Vietnam in December. The armed services decide to try to recruit more women.

1969   The secret bombing of Cambodia begins in March. On June 8, President Nixon announces the beginning of Vietnamization. About 25,000 American soldiers will be withdrawn from Vietnam. Massive antiwar demonstrations take place in Washington, D.C., in October and November. Red Cross volunteers begin their "Write Hanoi" campaign. More than 60,000 American soldiers are withdrawn from Vietnam by December 31.

1970   Secret negotiations between America and North Vietnam start in February. In April, American forces attack Cambodia. Antiwar demonstrations increase. Four students are killed at Kent State on May 4. American troop strength stands at 280,000 in December.

1971   In February, South Vietnamese troops begin assaults on the Ho Chi Minh trail in Laos to cut off supplies to the Viet Cong. The *New York Times* and the *Washington Post* publish the Pentagon Papers in June. American troops number 140,000 in December.

1972   Nixon is reelected in November. Peace talks break down in December.

1973   Peace talks resume in January, and an agreement is reached. The last of the American troops leave in March. Last POWs are freed in April.

1974   Fighting between North and South Vietnam resumes in January.

1975   The North Vietnamese begin their final offensive. The South Vietnamese army retreats in disarray. The last Americans are evacuated on April 29. Saigon falls on April 30.

1976   North and South Vietnam are united as one Communist nation.

1982   The Vietnam Veterans Memorial is unveiled on November 11.

1984   Vietnam Women's Memorial Project is established.

1993   Vietnam Women's Memorial is dedicated on November 11.

NOTES

Chapter One

1. Major General Jeanne Holm, *Women in the Military: An Unfinished Revolution* (Novato, Calif.: Presidio, 1992), p. 231.

2. Kathryn Marshall, *In the Combat Zone: An Oral History of American Women in Vietnam* (Boston: Little, Brown, 1987), p. 131.

3. Doris C. O'Neil, *The '60s* (Boston: Little, Brown, 1989), p. 203.

4. Rosalind Rosenberg, *Divided Lives: American Women in the Twentieth Century* (New York: Hill and Wang, 1992), p. 79.

5. Tom Shachtman, *Decade of Shocks: Dallas to Watergate, 1963–1974* (New York: Poseidon Press, 1983), pp. 243, 244.

Chapter Two

1. Miriam Frank, Marilyn Ziebarth, and Connie Field, *The Life and Times of Rosie the Riveter* (Emeryville, Calif.: Clarity Educational Productions, 1982), p. 23.

2. William B. Breuer, *War and American Women: Heroism, Deeds, and Controversy* (Westport, Conn.: Praeger, 1997), p. 71.

3. Breuer, p. 74.

4. Major General Jeanne Holm, *Women in the Military: An Unfinished Revolution* (Novato, Calif.: Presidio, 1992), p. 210.

5. Lois Decker O'Neill, editor, *The Women's Book of World Records and Achievements* (Garden City, N.Y.: Anchor Press/Doubleday, 1979), p. 539.

6. Keith Walker, *A Piece of My Heart: The Stories of Twenty-six American Women Who Served in Vietnam* (Novato, Calif.: Presidio Press, 1985), p. 27.

7. Walker, p. ix.

Chapter Three

1. Barry Denenberg, *Voices from Vietnam* (New York: Scholastic, 1995), p. 202.

2. Major General Jeanne Holm, *Women in the Military: An Unfinished Revolution* (Novato, Calif.: Presidio, 1992), p. 227.

3. Elizabeth Norman, *Women at War: The Story of Fifty Military Nurses Who Served in Vietnam* (Philadelphia: University of Pennsylvania Press, 1990), p. 88.

4. Keith Walker, *A Piece of My Heart: The Stories of Twenty-six American Women Who Served in Vietnam* (Novato, Calif.: Presidio Press, 1985), p. 217.

5. Norman, p. 111.

6. Denenberg, p. 200.

Chapter Four

1. Keith Walker, *A Piece of My Heart: The Stories of Twenty-six American Women Who Served in Vietnam* (Novato, Calif.: Presidio Press, 1985), p. 126.

2. Michael E. Stevens, *Voices of the Wisconsin Past: Voices from Vietnam* (Madison: State Historical Society of Wisconsin, 1996), pp. 140, 141.

3. Kathryn Marshall, *In the Combat Zone: An Oral History of American Women in Vietnam* (Boston: Little, Brown, 1987), p. 177.

4. Walker, p. 276.

5. Marshall, pp. 151–155

6. Walker, p. 179.

7. Walker, p. 181.

Chapter Five

1. Horst Fass and Tim Page, editors, *Requiem: By the Photographers Who Died in Vietnam and Indochina* (New York: Random House, 1997), p. 136.

2. Kay Mills, *A Place in the News: From the Women's Pages to the Front Page* (New York: Dodd, Mead & Company, 1988), p. 205.

3. Liz Trotta, *Fighting for Air: In the Trenches with Television News* (New York: Simon and Schuster, 1991), p. 57.

4. Trotta, p. 124.

5. Trotta, p. 125.

Chapter Six

1. Peter Davies, *The Truth About Kent State: A Challenge to the American Conscience* (New York: Farrar Straus Giroux, 1973), p. 7.

2. Tom Wells, *The War Within: America's Battle Over Vietnam* (Berkeley: University of California Press, 1994), p. 444.

3. Wells, p. 123.

4. Barbara L. Tischler, editor, *Sights on the Sixties* (New Brunswick, N.J.: Rutgers University Press, 1992), p. 180.

5. Clark Dougan and Samuel Lipsman, *The Vietnam Experience: A Nation Divided* (Boston: Boston Publishing Company, 1984), p. 177.

6. Thomas Powers, *The War at Home: Vietnam and the American People, 1964–1968* (Boston: G.K. Hall & Co., 1984), p. 199.

7. Heather Brandon, *Casualties: Death in Viet Nam, Anguish and Survival in America* (New York: St. Martin's Press, 1984), pp. 317, 331.

8. Don Luce and John Sommer, *Viet Nam: The Unheard Voices* (Ithaca, N.Y.: Cornell University Press), 1969, pp. 317–318.

Afterword

1. Elizabeth Norman, *Women at War: The Story of Fifty Military Nurses Who Served in Vietnam* (Philadelphia: University of Pennsylvania Press, 1990), p. 114.

2. Barry Denenberg, *Voices from Vietnam* (New York: Scholastic, 1995), p. 184.

3. Denenberg, p. 186.

FURTHER READING

To learn more about what women's lives were like during the Vietnam War, check out Volumes 9 and 10 in *The Young Oxford History of Women in the United States* series, *Pushing the Limits: American Women 1940–1961* by Elaine May (New York: Oxford University Press, 1994), and *The Road to Equality: American Women Since 1962* by William H. Chafe (New York: Oxford University Press, 1994).

To learn more about the war itself, read *The Vietnam War* by Roger Barr (San Diego: Lucent Books, 1991). This heavily illustrated book discusses the causes of the war, America's involvement in the conflict, and the price that Americans paid for participating in the struggle. Another excellent source for information about the war is a four-part series by David K. Wright, who served in Vietnam. *Eve of Battle*, *A Wider War*, *Vietnamization*, and *The Fall of Vietnam* (Children's Press, 1989) give detailed accounts of the ebb and flow of the war. These books are illustrated, and they also have comprehensive timelines.

To learn more about the women who were against the war, read *Jane Fonda: Political Activism* by Russell Shorto (The Millbrook Press, 1991), *Tinker v. Des Moines: Student Protest* by Leah Farish (Enslow, 1997), and *Coretta Scott King* by Lisa Rhodes (Chelsea House, 1998).

It took years for Americans to come to grips with the horrors of the war in Vietnam and the incredible losses it had inflicted. Anger, frustration, and bitterness prevented the public from erecting memorials to those who had served during the conflict. It wasn't until almost twenty years after the war ended that the Vietnam Women's Memorial was dedicated. To learn more about the story behind this memorial, read Deborah Kent's book, *The Vietnam Women's Memorial* (Children's Press, 1995).

INDEX